26X 9/05v12/05

20X5/02v7/02

JUN 20 2000

trade stocks online

WILEY ONLINE TRADING FOR A LIVING

Electronic Day Trading to Win / Bob Baird and Craig McBurney

The Strategic Electronic Day Trader / Robert Deel

Day Trade Online / Christopher A. Farrell

Trade Options Online / George A. Fontanills

Electronic Day Trading 101 / Sunny J. Harris

Trade Stocks Online / Mark L. Larson

How I Trade for a Living / Gary Smith

trade stocks online

MARK L. LARSON

John Wiley & Sons, Inc.

New York • Chichester • Weinheim • Brisbane • Singapore • Toronto

Published by John Wiley & Sons, Inc.
Published simultaneously in Canada.

This publication is designed to provide accurate and authoritative information in regard to the subject matter covered. It is sold with the understanding that the publisher is not engaged in rendering professional services. If professional advice or other expert assistance is required, the services of a competent professional person should be sought.

Charts in this book, unless noted, were produced by TeleChart 2000, which is a registered trademark of Worden Brothers, Inc., Five Oaks Office Park, 4905 Pine Cone Drive, Durham, NC 27707, (800) 776-4940 or (919) 408-0542, www.tc2000.com.

Library of Congress Cataloging-in-Publication Data:

Larson, Mark.
    Trade stocks online / Mark Larson.
        p. cm. — (Wiley online trading for a living)
    Includes index.
    ISBN 0-471-38473-9 (alk. paper)
        1. Day trading (Securities)   2. Investments—Computer network resources.
    I. Title.   II. Series.

    HG4515.95 .L37 2000
    332.64'2'0285—dc21

                                                                99-059988

Printed in the United States of America.

10 9 8 7 6 5 4 3 2 1

preface

The preface of any book is a place of decisions. One will usually scan the preface while standing beside a bookstand and then turn to the back cover to see the cost of the book. Let me ask you: How does one determine if the cost of the book is worth the contents of the text? Wouldn't you say that it would be determined on the basis of what knowledge was obtained from reading the book?

The information that I have provided in this book can change your life! Knowledge, skills, and experience have been acquired from some of the most successful traders in the stock market and are condensed in the following pages to show you how to dramatically increase your income and have more free time.

My purpose in writing this book is to help others change their lives, not only for themselves, but also so they can pass

---

Every morning, I get up and look through the Forbes list of the richest people in America. If I'm not there, I go to work.

—Robert Orben

on the knowledge to their families and friends. For some it may be a determining factor that increases their income by an additional few hundred dollars a month, and for others it may be the difference of thousands of dollars a day.

Each chapter is written with as much simplicity as possible so that the average person, like myself, can understand it. Chapter after chapter, you will experience my enthusiasm and passion for the path toward the dream of *financial independence*.

In the beginning chapters, I explain in detail how to treat the stock market like a business. I show you six different money-making opportunities that utilize stock-split investing. I cover long-term investments using options on LEAPS, and also explain how to sell calls against stocks or options. In the final chapter, I show you an extremely powerful cash-rewarding strategy known on Wall Street as *bull put spreads*. You will see how the power of matching more than one strategy to another can capture an even greater return on your money.

This preface is being written as an afterthought to assure you, the reader, that you absolutely will get your money's worth. I hope that, after reading this book, you will choose to utilize the information of specialized knowledge to help you change your life and to better understand ways of investing in the stock market.

May you be blessed tenfold, as I have been, and be able to give to others as others have given to me. I hope you will read on with passion, enthusiasm, encouragement, and confidence, and will enjoy taking the journey with me down Wall Street.

MARK L. LARSON
San Francisco, California

Dream to be more than what you are.

—Keith D. Harrell

acknowledgments

This book would have only been a thought if it hadn't been for the people in my life who have, in some way, been an inspiration to me. Not only by their help and support in the form of knowledge, but by their support and words of encouragement, they have taught me not to give up but instead to make my dreams come true.

And to all of my wonderful family members—Mom, Dad, Brothers, Sister, Grandfather, Aunt Julie, Uncle Jim, Rick, Verne Lind, and the world's greatest friends—thank you all for your love and support when I was willing to give up. All of your loving support has allowed me to dust off my lifelong dreams and turn them into reality.

And most of all, a special loving thanks to my girlfriend, Tamara Olea, not only for your moral support, but as well for

---

*To love is to cherish, as cherish is to love those
who stand by your side.*

—Mark Larson

making this book what it is. You are not only the greatest girl-friend, but also a wonderful teammate!

Dreams can become reality if you work at them, believe in yourself and trust in the Lord. May you all be blessed with love, passion, and happiness.

M. L. L.

Hope is a waking dream.

—Aristotle

contents

trade
stocks
online

chapter 1

the financial dream

Have you ever caught yourself daydreaming of flying off to a faraway tropical island for a nice long vacation in the sun? Now, visualize again with me for a moment. You're a young child, full of life, you can climb the highest tree and reach the farthest star. Nothing is impossible!

As a child you might have said things like, "When I grow up I'm going to become a doctor and have a lot of money," or "I'm going to own a big house and drive a Ferrari." Unfortunately, as we grow older we begin to realize that our childhood dreams can be very disappointing. We begin to understand that nice things cost a lot of money, and the American Dream

---

When I was young, I used to think that money was the most important thing in life; now that I am old, I know it is.

—Oscar Wilde

becomes just that, a dream. The cost of living begins to change our outlook on life and our dreams seem to fade away as reality sets in.

My hat goes off to those of you who have gone on to become successful and live in a big house and have the Ferrari in your driveway. But, unfortunately, for most people, childhood dreams never become reality. We find ourselves having to work harder and harder and longer and longer just to pay the required bills of everyday living. The cost of living somehow seems to increase faster than our wages do.

Wages are based on your income, and your income is based on your time. For thousands of people, their time is their only source of income. Meaning that if they choose not to go to work, their income *stops*. Nicely put, they are trading their time for a paycheck. Their time is their income-producing asset. If you are your only source of income, what will happen to your income if your asset doesn't go to work? It will stop, yet the cost of living will continue on.

As we mature and embark on our journey through life, we can't help but wonder about all the different challenges that can and will affect our lives. Many things happen in our lives that we could never have anticipated. And by the same token, many things happen because we make them happen.

I would like to reflect back for a moment on the year 1997. I was 31 years old and felt that I was on top of the world, when I unexpectedly found myself in the middle of a traumatic financial downfall. After working so hard to acquire all of my assets (apartment buildings, duplexes, and businesses) I lost everything. My businesses were shut down and my property was taken away as I was forced to file for bankruptcy. I had invested in a large business venture and lost. May this be a lesson to

---

The worst bankruptcy in the world is the person who has lost enthusiasm.

—Ralph Waldo Emerson

you: Diversify and protect your assets. Never put all of your hard-earned money in one deal—and the same goes for the stock market.

When I was given the opportunity to learn strategies for investing in the stock market I was very skeptical, especially after losing everything. As a successful real estate agent for 12 years, I had represented hundreds of real estate investors who had made and lost fortunes in the stock market. Later I found that it not only did not take a lot of money to be an investor but also that those investors had lost money only due to their lack of knowledge.

I share my personal misfortune with you solely so that as you read through each chapter, you will realize that average people (like me) with an average income (or, in my case, no income) can still obtain the American Dream.

What is your financial dream? For me, it is being able to do whatever I want to do whenever I want to do it. The stock market has allowed me to have financial freedom, which allows me the time to spend with my family, friends, and church, and, most important, to help those who are less fortunate.

The stock market is a wonderful place to make a living, as thousands do throughout the world. When treated like a business the stock market can dramatically change your life, as it has mine. Thanks to the stock market, I have realized that the dream of financial independence is alive and doing well.

The strategies covered in this book are not new, but to many of you they will seem very different. By taking time to learn, you have taken one more step forward toward learning how to properly earn more returns more often. These concepts are the same concepts that have enabled me to dust off my life-long dreams and retire from ever *having* to work again.

The reason most of us don't live within our income
is that we don't consider that living.

—Joe Moore

I dedicate this section of the book to those of you who are retired and are able to relate to it. Our government has brainwashed most people into the 65-year retirement plan by enticing us to think that it is the only way to safely retire. The discounted tax shelters such as the 401(k)s, mutual funds, and many others may be enough for some people, but not for me. I don't buy the government's theory that I would be able to retire with financial security if I were to put all of my hard-earned money into a retirement fund. That's almost as bad as counting on Social Security as your only source of income. If the plan our government has in place for us works so well, then why is it that 90 percent of all Americans have to downsize their lifestyle when they retire? My grandfather is one of the 90 percent, who, like thousands of others, bought into the 65-year program and contributed his hard-earned money. Unfortunately, today, as a retired person with a dual income, he has had to downsize his lifestyle and closely manage his retirement income.

The problem with the government's plan is:

- The rates of return on your investments are *too low.*
- You have to be retired before enjoying your retirement money.
- There is no guarantee of what your investments will be worth when you retire.

The biggest problem with the idea of retiring at the age of 65 is not just having to wait to enjoy your money, but the lack of time you have to enjoy it. Most people don't live past 70 years of age. Now that's an encouraging thought! We work hard every day until we're 65 years old, and then have only approx-

---

Plans are nothing, planning is everything.

—Dwight D. Eisenhower

imately 5 years to enjoy our lifelong investments. The true definition of retirement should be, "Retired from working, but not retired from *making money*." This redefined definition is why, at the age of 34, I no longer have to trade my time for a paycheck if I choose not to. I could write an entire book on our government's retirement plans—or, shall I say, lack of plans—but let's stay focused on your financial dream and not your broker's or the government's. There are many reasons why people invest in the stock market. Here are a few:

- Retirement
- Children's college tuition
- Tax shelters (that's a joke)
- Bequeathment (to pass assets on to their church and loved ones)

My concern with this reasoning is that you may need the investment money sooner, and there is no guarantee that your investments will be worth more than they were when you originally invested. Proper personal planning and investment education will help you make better financial decisions. Your financial knowledge will determine your true net worth and let *you* decide when to retire.

You will learn throughout this book that I, too, believe in long-term investments—the difference is that I believe in selling them when there is a profit to be made. Treating the stock market like a business may be an entirely new concept for many people. The number-one, and most important, rule is to get good at *selling,* not *holding.* Businesses make money only when they sell something for a profit and then reinvest again.

Who is speaking of victory? To survive is everything.

—Rainer Maria Rilke

chapter 2

trading is
a business

You will learn throughout this book that the idea is to treat your investments like a business by determining your profit before the initial investment takes place. Treating the stock market like a business may be an entirely new concept for many people. The tough part for any investor is to understand that you need to get good at *selling.*

For most of you this may be a different approach. We have been raised listening to others say it is wise to buy stock and hold on to it for the long haul. The question is, "How long should you hold on to an investment?" The obvious answer is, "Until you make a profit." But just how much of a profit? I'll leave that up to you to decide. Personally, I like

---

Everyone lives by selling something.

—Robert Louis Stevenson

to make from $500 to $1,500 a day. Of course, this isn't done every trading day.

No matter what your purpose for investing may be, your returns will ultimately be based on having specialized knowledge. That means knowing how to make money when the market goes up, down, or sideways.

As I refer to the stock market as a business, you will need to understand the concept behind that characterization. By doing so, you will learn that your stock market investments can be very rewarding.

As with any business, the first requirement is self-discipline. This means setting goals and knowing what you want to get out of your investment. It also means knowing how to get what you want so you won't have to leave your future up to your stockbroker. In other words, learn as much as you can so that you can be the best at what you do.

Knowledge is the key to wealth. It is the *right* knowledge that is important, not just any kind of knowledge. Why do you suppose people focus on a major in college? For most people, it is to gain specialized knowledge and to enhance their career in a certain field of employment. Some people will even go on to private schooling to acquire even more knowledge or to get an edge on the competition.

As with any profession or business, you must dedicate hours to studying and research, and have the required amount of money to get started. The stock market can be a scary place, and that is why it is so important to treat it like a business. The idea is to turn your investments into profits. Do not think of it as a way to get rich quick.

You will learn throughout this book that the idea is to determine your profit before the initial investment ever takes place.

The more we study, the more we discover our ignorance.

—Percy Bysshe Shelley

To explain the theory of treating the stock market like a business, I will compare it to the popular company Home Depot (HD). Before going into business, the specialists at Home Depot probably researched such things as supply and demand, wholesale versus retail costs, and so on. They then most likely went on to purchase products they felt would be valuable to the customers and profitable for the company, and then offered those items to the public. In other words, their goal was to go from *cash* to *asset* to *cash.* The idea is to buy at wholesale (low) and sell at retail (higher), making small (or large) profits by doing so.

Home Depot, like thousands of other businesses, is in business to make a lot of little profits. If they shelved a product that wasn't selling in a reasonable amount of time, they would probably discount the product to get their investment back and go on to reinvest in another product that was in greater demand. You won't go broke by making a lot of little profits, but it could be a different story if you invested only according to the buy and hold theory.

Selling versus Holding

Think of your investment in the stock market as being the same as owning a retail store. Would you go home for the evening and leave the doors of the store open for anyone to take your money and assets? Of course not! You need to pay close attention to your business, whether it be a retail store or the stock market. If you manage your business with the intent of creating more revenue, you are sure to be successful.

So, let's say you have $2,500 to open your business (your trading account). You need to make wise decisions in order to increase your premium. The key to treating the stock market

I'm no good in permanent positions. My feet go to sleep.

—Kevin Costner

like a business is to make wholesale investments and sell them for a profit.

Money on the Table Spells *Trouble*

Take companies such as Microsoft (MSFT), Dell Computer (DELL), or even Lucent Technologies (LU). In the past their stock has continued to climb, but anything is possible. The stock can go down just as fast as, if not faster than, it went up. Any kind of bad news can have a dramatic effect on a company's stock value. This is why some investors do not like to leave their money "on the table" over the weekend. Anything can, and does, happen over those two days, which can gap the stock value down overnight—a perfect reason to buy and sell rather than buy and hold.

In my opinion, there are benefits to owning long-term stock, but only when writing covered calls against it to collect a monthly premium. This goes back to having specialized knowledge in order to understand how to earn the maximum return on your investments.

If you were to look back into your security investments, I'm sure you would notice that there have been times when the value has dropped. Use any of the past stock market crashes (or *pullbacks,* as I prefer) as an example. The value of almost all stocks dropped, which enabled those investors who didn't have all of their money tied up in buy-and-hold stock to purchase blue-chip stocks at an incredible wholesale price. My point here is not to belittle anyone; I am merely stressing the fact that you need to treat your investments like a business.

If you bet a horse, that's gambling. If you bet you can make three spades, that's entertainment. If you bet cotton will go up three points, that's business. See the difference?

—William F. Sherrod

Be in Control of Your Money

For many people, the term *stock market investing* means one thing—losing money. Some people have even gone as far to say that it is no different from gambling in Las Vegas, except you don't get the free dinner show. This statement is partially true if *you* are not in control. The idea is to be *in control* of your money. Do your homework, educate yourself, and don't rely on a broker to make investment decisions for you. After all, it's *your* money. Brokers make money whether you win or lose. I have a great broker, but I make all the decisions, because I have the knowledge and my best interests in mind.

Rules to Trade By

> *Rule 1:* Don't get greedy. Make an investment, take a small profit and move on. You can't go broke by taking a lot of small profits.

> *Rule 2:* Get good at buying wholesale and selling retail. By doing this you are sure to generate a profit. Remember, cash to asset to cash.

> Rule 3: Always determine your exit points before making any trade, whether it be for a profit or a loss.

If you're going to treat the stock market like a business, then consistently use the three rules of business success.

Commissions

Due to today's technology, an investor has the capability to place trades with several different types of brokerage firms: *full*

To open a business is very easy; to keep it open is very difficult.

—Chinese proverb

service, discount, deep discount, and, of course, *online brokers.* I use several different brokerage firms for my business, depending on the type of trade being made. When playing a fast, "newsy" trade, I need to call the full-service broker to be assured that my order has been filled immediately. The full-service broker also allows me to be in business from anywhere in the country, as long as I have a cell phone and their toll-free 800 number.

Online services are great for all types of investing. And as time goes on, we investors will be offered more opportunities. Even today, online services offer individual investors the capability to directly place trades on the Nasdaq exchange. This is done with a Level 2 screen, which is used for day trading.

Choose a broker that meets your personality and needs, but more so your expense requirements (commission budget). I use a full-service broker and an online account, but my commissions with my full-service broker are negotiable, which gives me the type of service I expect at the cost of a deep-discount broker. Many people ask why a broker would discount the commissions. Investors who treat the stock market like a business do a lot more buying and selling. This generates a lot more trades, which, overall, rewards the broker with a lot more profits than are generated by the average investor who buys and holds. My average commission cost on 1,000 shares of stock, regardless of stock price, is $40 to $80 a trade. When trading options with E. D. & F. Man in Chicago (800-837-6212), my average commission for 10 contracts is $50.

Online accounts vary in many ways, so do not let a cheaper price be the deciding factor as to which service you will use. It is important to use a service that gives you quick

---

It is more admirable to be in business for yourself than to work for somebody else.

—H. L. Mencken

telephone service (with a toll-free 800 number). If you haven't experienced this already, there are days when online systems go down, as computers will from time to time, so give yourself the flexibility of not having to rely on your computer or the Internet to make a trade. The best way to research online accounts is by viewing the different advantages and disadvantages of each firm. A wonderful online site to research this information is www.gomez.com. This site does a great job of making information available so you can decide which account is best for you and your business needs.

As I have said several times, you as the investor should always be in complete control of your investments, and that means the bookkeeping aspects, as well. I place an average of 15 to 20 trades a month, and since both the broker and myself are human, it is inevitable that mistakes will be made from time to time. Bookkeeping is just as important as the trade itself. So you must get as good at bookkeeping as you are at trading.

I find it easier to track my trades daily rather than waiting until the end of the month to balance my statement. In order to do so, I carry a stack of small index cards with me, and after I place a trade, I write all the details of the trade onto the index card. I now have a tracking system that goes wherever I go—not only am I able to be in business anywhere at any time, but I'm able to react to any market condition, as long as I have current information regarding my investments at hand. At this very moment, I am checking my index cards as the stock market is up 110 points, about to break the new Dow high. Seeing that the market is bullish today, I need to review my trading positions to see if it's time to sell for a profit.

After I close a position for a profit, and I've completed all of the written information on the index card, I file the card in

---

I believe that the power to make money is a gift from God.

—John D. Rockefeller

my closed trades file and wait to receive my confirmation slips in the mail. I then match both ends of the trade (buy and sell) with the confirmation slips received from my broker. They do not always match, and the difference is usually in the commissions. The commissions aren't always what I expected; sometimes they are lower, so I will make it a point to thank my broker. This also makes my broker aware that I am double-checking each trade.

After the index cards are matched up with the confirmation slips, they are filed weekly, then monthly, and yearly. This system enables me to match all of my business trades with each daily, monthly, and yearly statement received from the brokerage firm. And finally, it's off to the accountant with an organized tracking system along with all of the business expenses.

Since I am treating this as a business, I must make all of the investment transactions through a business, a *corporate* business (a Nevada corporation). Trading in the stock market is not the only purpose for incorporating. Another advantage is that the list of corporate officers is not required to be disclosed to the Internal Revenue Service or to any private individuals. The profits made in the corporate trading account are taxed at a corporate rate rather than an individual rate. And because the corporate office is located in Nevada, the corporation pays no state tax.

This is a serious business, as your financial investments should rightly be, so structure your business properly. The average investor will pay about 30 to 40 percent of all yearly profits in taxes, while a corporate investor in Nevada pays much less, even before deducting all the corporate expenses.

Good actions ennoble us, and we are the sons
of our own deeds.

—Miguel de Cervantes

These expenses are for the individual (who shall remain anonymous) who needs a car allowance, business traveling expenses (as he travels to such places as Hawaii, considering future investments), medical insurance, a computer, a cell phone, and several other expenses related to the corporation's investments.

Let me clarify that I am by no means a tax advisor or accountant in any shape or form, nor do I have specialized knowledge about the tax laws—I leave that part of the business to my tax attorney. You'll learn that good tax attorneys are worth their pay. The important thing to keep in mind about taxes is not how little you have to pay now, but rather, how little you will have to pay at the time of retirement. Remember the old saying, "Always cover your assets!"

The most popular labor-saving device is still money.

—Phyllis George

chapter 3

discipline for trading

Discipline is the key to becoming a successful investor. A great example of discipline is control. You need to be able to properly control your emotions, as well as your profits and losses. This chapter will show you several ways to discipline yourself in this business. By following all of the steps, you will learn to discipline your trading habits, and in doing so, you will become a better investor and will be able to reward yourself with financial independence.

Specialized knowledge is an important key to success. I have dedicated many years to studying the stock market to become as knowledgeable as possible. Each and every day I strive to read more, practice more, and study harder.

Let no man value at a little price a virtuous woman's counsel.

—George Chapman

This is a small price to pay for financial independence. Most college graduates dedicate at least four years to acquiring their specialized knowledge. The importance of specialized knowledge is in knowing how to react to any market condition—knowing how to control your ability to make money when the market goes up, when it goes sideways, and especially when it goes down.

Having the right tools also enhances your trading ability. All professions have certain required tools. A surgeon needs a scalpel, just as a pilot needs a plane. An investor needs the following tools to be effective: a charting service (such as TeleChart 2000), a paging service, a cell phone, and a good computer. All of these tools are essential to successful trading. You may use a different service than the one listed here; it is given only as an example.

Investment Partner

Another helpful tool is an investment partner. This person should be someone who can assist you in making educated decisions—and I'm not referring to your stock broker. I'm referring to a family member, friend, business partner, or, better yet, a group of masterminds who do the same thing you do—people who invest for a living.

My girlfriend and I make a great team. She sees things from a different point of view. She is much more conservative than I am. She will see a $500 profit, take the profit, and find another trade, whereas I myself have a tendency to get greedy. But remember, cash to asset to cash.

I not only use all the brains I have, but all I can borrow.

—Woodrow Wilson

When I've questioned both men and women to see who would be willing to take a sure $500 profit over a chance for more money, inevitably 9 out of 10 women said they would be happy taking the $500. I have no proven study as to why women are more conservative when it comes to collecting a profit; maybe it is their natural maternal instincts. Simply put, men who have female partners tend to have more discipline than those who do not. Admit it, guys—you know we were all out of control with no true direction until our spouses came along and put us in line with the future! I'm sure you can relate to driving down the road with your wife or girlfriend and getting lost. She suggests you stop at a gas station for directions. Of course, your macho ego kicks in, and you won't do it, because you'll find your way, *eventually.* Swallow your pride and acquire a little maternal instinct and your trading habits will be more profitable.

As the old saying goes, "Two heads are better than one." I greatly enjoy working with my girlfriend. It's great to have the same interests and talk about our business—the stock market. Why shouldn't both you and your spouse also enjoy the financial fruits of not only making money, but having more free time for each other and your family? Having her as a business partner enables me to travel as I teach others to become financially independent, because she manages our business while I'm on the road.

Paper Trading

We all have heard the saying, "Practice makes perfect." Well, I am going to tell you that statement is untrue. It should read,

---

Dollars do better if they are accompanied by sense.

—Earl Riney

"Perfect practice makes perfect." You could practice something the wrong way over and over again, but if you don't practice it the right way it will never be perfect. So, when it comes to investing in the stock market, I want you to perfectly practice with white money before using green money—start out with *paper trading*. Get good at paper trading a strategy without using any money, and practice until you consistently have more winners than you do losers. Then you will be ready to start using the green money (cash). Use the following checklist for all your trades.

The proper way to paper trade is to determine the following:

- Why are you investing in this particular company?
- What will the cost of the investment be?
- What price have you decided to sell it at on the upside?
- What price are you willing to sell it at for a loss?

After you have committed yourself to a paper trade, follow through with it as you would with a real trade. After the play is over, whether you win or lose, figure out your rate of return on your investment. This completes a perfect paper trade.

Rate of Return

First, let me explain what *rate of return* means. It is the percentage of profit from an investment. What is the average rate of return on most long-term investments? 10, 20, 30 percent annually? I would like to go on record as saying that the average rate of return for most Americans is *low,* as in too low.

---

*Success generally depends on knowing how long
it takes to succeed.*

—Montesquieu

Many people think that 30 percent is a great annual rate of return. I assure you that if you think that even 30 percent is a great annual return, you won't by the end of this book. In fact, you'll probably delete the words *annual return* from your vocabulary.

The following is an example of a monthly rate of return:

Selling price	$7,000
Original investment	$5,000
Profit	$2,000

$$\text{Monthly return} = \frac{\$2,000}{\$5,000} = 40\%$$

Annual return = 40% × 12 months = 480%

Now, that is a nice annual return! The original investment was $5,000. The money was invested for 1 month and sold for $7,000, netting a $2,000 profit. I divided the profit by the original investment and came up with a percentage, 40 percent. Then, assuming that I could make the same conservative investment month after month for the next year (multiplying the monthly return by 12) gives me a 480 percent annual return.

This example is very realistic and can be done monthly. Some investments will net you less profit, and then again, some investments will net you more. My point is, whether it be 10, 20, 30 percent, or more monthly, give yourself a greater yearly return.

The key to figuring your rate of return is in selling your investments, which obviously is very different in concept from the buy-and-hold theory. You need to get in the habit of turning cash into profits and back to cash. Sell, sell, sell!

Only a fool holds out for the top dollar.

—Joseph P. Kennedy

Selling

Wal-Mart (WMT) is in business to make money and be success-ful, which they have been for many, many years. What makes a business successful? They are good at selling for a profit. Whether it be merchandise or a stock or option, you need to get good at buying at wholesale and selling at retail.

Wal-Mart would not be successful if they bought a prod-uct, put it on the shelves, and locked the doors, hoping that someday in the future, when they needed more money, they could sell their product for a profit. So why should investors do business that way?

Knowing When to Exit

You need to predetermine when to sell your investment for a profit and, even more important, what price to sell at if you have to take a loss.

In elementary school, we learned and practiced the fire drill. At any moment an emergency could occur, and we needed to know how to safely and calmly exit the building. The same goes for the stock market. Don't put your money at risk by not knowing where to exit.

A *good-till-canceled* (GTC) order is a tool that may be used not only to sell (close out) a position, but also to buy (open) a position. After buying stock or options, I place a GTC order at my predetermined sell price. By doing so, I automatically set a price at which I will sell my stock or option.

Most brokerage firms allow a GTC order to remain in force

Man is a tool-using animal . . . without tools he is nothing, with tools he is all.

—Thomas Carlyle

for up to 60 days. Make sure you clarify this with your broker. It is important to always determine your sell price as soon as you have received the confirmation of your purchase.

Example

Stock

| Buy 1,000 shares at $7 | $7,000 |
| Set a GTC order to sell at $8 | $1,000 profit |

Option

| Buy 10 contracts at $3 | $3,000 |
| Set a GTC order to sell at $4. | $1,000 profit |

Now that you understand the purpose of a GTC order, I'd like you to note that GTC is also an acronym for *get the cash.* When you place a GTC order to sell for a higher price, keep in mind that you predetermined that sell price to make a profit. So take the profit!

As time goes on, you will become greedy and raise your GTC order to make more money. When the greed sets in, your profits will most likely go down, not up. So when you find yourself getting greedy, remember that GTC means *get the cash.*

Stop-Loss Order

Stop-loss orders are used to predetermine your exit point on the downside of an investment. They act as a safety net. In other words, they provide an exit point when you are wrong and have misjudged the direction of the stock or option.

Nothing in life is to be feared. It is only to be understood.

—Marie Curie

We invest for a purpose, and when the investment performs to our advantage we take our profits, but when an investment goes against us, we need to know how far we are going to allow our investment to drop before we sell it.

There are several ways to determine what dollar amount you may choose to lose before cutting your loss. GTC orders are used when selling for a profit on the upside and stop losses are used when selling for a loss on the downside. When placing a trade, it is a wise decision to implement both a GTC order and a stop-loss order together.

Example

Stock

Buy 1,000 shares at $7	$7,000
Place a GTC order at $8	$1,000 profit
Place a stop-loss order at $6	$1,000 loss

This is a wise trade. The stock market is very volatile, and a stock can go up just as well as it can go down, in just a matter of seconds. By utilizing a GTC order and a stop loss, you have enabled yourself to go on with your day knowing that at any time during the next 60 days you could sell your stock for a profit. And on the other hand, in case the stock drops below $6, you have agreed to sell it at $6.

One thing you should know is that stop losses are not allowed on all exchanges. If they are not allowed, I have my broker put the stock on a computer and order it to activate an alarm at my desired loss price. If the stock drops down to my sell price, the system alerts the broker with a ringing sound, and the broker sells my stock.

Set all things in their own peculiar place, and know that order is the greatest grace.

—John Dryden

Remember, this is all about discipline, and if you properly follow the three-step process, you should come out with a rewarding profit.

Three-Step Process

1. Gather information.
2. Analyze the information.
3. React.

If a trade does not go in the direction you had planned, move on to the next trade. Try not to let the loss bother you; after all, you can't win on every trade. And I assure you that there will even be times when you will see the stock go back up in price after you have sold it for a loss, but more often than not, it will drop even lower, and you will be happy that you had your stop loss.

A *one cancels the other* (OCO) order is used when you have placed a GTC order and a stop-loss order. It simply means that you have agreed that if your GTC order is filled, then your stop-loss order will be canceled. Or, vice versa, if the stop-loss order is activated, then your GTC order will be canceled. Always make sure that the second order is canceled; otherwise, you may end up putting yourself in a position of having to sell something that you have already sold.

Trailing Stop Loss

Trailing stop losses are also highly effective when implemented. A trailing stop loss is no more than a stop loss that trails up as your profits move higher.

Quit while you're ahead. All the best gamblers do.

—Baltasar Gracián

Example

Buy stock at $6.

Place a GTC order to sell at $7.

Place a stop-loss order at $5.

As the stock moves up to $6.50, place your trailing stop loss at a higher price ($5.50 or $6.00). If you realize that your investment can move above your GTC order, you may choose to cancel the GTC order and allow the trailing stop loss to determine what price to sell at. This is determined as you continuously move your stop loss higher, trailing the upward movement of the stock price. Now you are allowing the stock's momentum to determine when to sell for a greater profit. Let's say the stock traded as high as $8.00 and you continuously moved your stop loss up to the price of $7.75. If the stock dropped back down to $7.75, then your trailing stop loss would have enabled you to sell your stock for the higher profit of $7.75 instead of your original GTC order of $7.00. I don't consider this being greedy, merely maximizing your profits as a wise business investor.

GTC orders and stop losses are tools of the business. Brokerage firms should allow you to place them at no cost to you the investor. If your broker is from the old school, find a firm that allows you to properly protect your business investments.

When implementing GTC orders, stop losses, and trailing stop losses, you have to understand that *gapping* can have a positive or negative effect on the stock or option.

It is easier to do a job right than to explain why you didn't.

—Martin Van Buren

Gapping

Gapping occurs as a reaction to either good or bad news, causing the stock or option to open either higher or lower than the last traded price. If news on a company is released during market hours, the stock will be halted, creating a gap in the price when the stock reopens for trading. Upward gaps are common with announcements of good news such as positive earnings, stock splits, company takeovers, approval of a drug by the Food and Drug Administration (FDA), and so on.

Effect of Good News on a GTC Order—Upward Gap

In an upward gap, a stock or option opens at a higher price than its last trade. If the reopening price is higher than your set GTC order, then your sell order will be filled at the next trading price, which gives you even more of a profit.

Effect of Bad News on a Stop-Loss Order—Downward Gap

Just the opposite of an upward gap, bad news can gap a stock or option down in value. As with the upward gap, the downward gap usually occurs after market hours, or it may occur during market hours if the stock is halted. When the stock gaps down below your stop-loss order or trailing stop loss, you will receive the next lower trading price when the stock reopens for trading. If a downward gap occurs you will be happy you had your stop loss in place, as the stock could continue to drop lower in value, especially if the market is bearish for the day.

High ethical standards bring about efficient business methods.

—Watts

chapter 4

cashing in on the analysts

The stock market is unpredictable, with a lot of uncertainty. As you read on, you will learn that the key to making money is to play the individual stocks that are movers. By *movers,* I mean the stocks that are moving in a certain direction (either upward or downward) in reaction to the news from an analyst.

Brokerage firms have analysts who do nothing more than follow the performance of individual companies. A lot of time and hard work goes into their research. After a complete review of their findings, it is normal for the analysts or brokerage firm to make a public report on the information they have gathered. A large part of an analyst's research involves deter-

The greater thing in this world is not so much where we stand as in what direction we are going.

—Oliver Wendell Holmes

mining whether a company is productive. This information is one of the deciding factors as to whether a company will report positive or negative earnings each quarter.

Companies release earnings quarterly; usually, companies that are in the same sector have a pattern of releasing their earnings at approximately the same time as their competitors. Earnings alone are the number-one reason why a stock will go up or down on a regular basis. A company must continue to have positive quarterly earnings if it plans to keep investors' interest. As a business becomes more and more profitable, investors tend to become more and more attracted to the company, which, in turn, drives the stock price up.

Many companies continue to show a loss of earnings year after year. These companies are found in the Internet and drug sectors, for example. Investors choose to invest in these companies with the anticipation that they will be profitable in the future. Examples for Internet stocks are those such as CMG Information Services, Inc. (CMGI), and Amazon.com (AMZN). Quarter after quarter they report a business loss—but the important key factor is that they report *less* of a loss each quarter. Because they lower their losses each quarter, investors believe that at some point in the future they will start to show a profit.

In the drug sector, losses usually occur during the start-up stages, as companies tend to spend money on the research of new drugs. Drug companies start to report positive earnings when the FDA approves their drugs, at which time the product can be marketed. Investors invest in these nonmoneymaking companies, based on the hype of what they might do in the future.

Action may not always bring happiness;
but there is no happiness without action.

—Benjamin Disraeli

No matter what companies you decide to invest in, be sure that they prove that they can make money somewhere in the future and, more important, that they continue to beat their previous earnings. If a company doesn't show a good track record of making money, remember that your *investment* may be more at risk than the future of a company that hasn't proven itself. Blue-chip stocks are highly held stocks simply because they continue to perform better financially. Many people consider these stocks a better investment. I consider any short-term profitable stock to be a good investment.

The bottom line is that you will find analysts putting their necks out on the line daily making the public aware of their feelings on how an individual stock should perform. Their opinions usually have an effect on the value of the stock, which causes the stock to move either up or down.

The Play

Prior to the market opening each morning, I listen to the analysts' information on CNBC. This system is great for me, mainly because I'm the type of individual that likes to be spoon-fed the headline news as fast as possible. I like to know that the information is coming from a research team of individuals who know what they're doing. I value their specialized knowledge. (The proof is in the profits.)

Once again, specialized knowledge is the key to making money in the market. Once you understand how to play any market direction, you apply that specialized knowledge and make the money. After my pager alerts me each trading morning, I follow the same three-step process as I would with any trade:

Knowledge is free at the library. Just bring your own container.

—Anonymous

1. Gather information.
2. Analyze the information.
3. Quickly react or not (that is, make the trade or decide not to).

I receive a lot of valuable market information from CNBC, as well as the analysts' opinions on which stocks are being upgraded and downgraded. This is the brokerage firm or analyst's opinion of how an individual company will perform.

As simple as it sounds, firms and analysts will upgrade a company if they are bullish. And the opposite is the downgrade, if the firms and analysts are bearish. This is the meaning of what are commonly known in the industry as upgrades and downgrades. Consider the characterization of being bullish or bearish on a company to be the same as being bullish or bearish on the overall market. Your daily decision to be bullish or bearish can reward you with a daily profit (cash to asset to cash).

The Who's Who of the Analysts

The who's who of Wall Street applies not only to the stocks on Wall Street, but also to the analysts on Wall Street. Just as a company builds a rapport with its investors, an analyst builds a rapport on Wall Street. A stock, to many, is attractive only when it is moving upward. Analysts are attractive only when they are right. We as investors are rewarded only when we have more winning trades than losing trades. (Analysts are rewarded in their employment when they are right more often than they are wrong.) Not all investors or analysts are always right, but usually they are right

---

When I've heard all I need to make a decision,
I don't take a vote, I make a decision.

—Ronald Reagan

in the majority of cases. Analysts are called analysts because they analyze information in detail. We, as investors, need to analyze our investment decisions as the analysts do.

As mentioned, not all analysts are right, but certain brokerage firms and analysts are more respected than others. Investors listen when they speak. Get good at knowing who's who, as the better analysts can have a larger impact on stock values. You'll find, as I do with my news pager, that certain analysts are more accurate in their observations; they are the analysts I choose to follow. These analysts are well-known brokerage firms such as A. G. Edwards, Alex. Brown, Bear Stearns, Goldman Sachs, Lehman Brothers, Merrill Lynch, Morgan Stanley Dean Witter, PaineWebber, Piper Jaffrey, Prudential Securities, and Salomon Smith Barney—commonly known as the big boys of the market (see Figure 4.1).

Is a *Buy* a Buy or a Sell?

Brokerage firms have several ratings of upgrades and downgrades, and a buy rating doesn't always mean you should buy the stock. It could simply mean that the stock was lowered from a higher rating to the lower rating, making it a buy. Understanding the ratings and how a rating can affect a stock can mean the difference in how much money you make. Such firms as PaineWebber, Salomon Smith Barney, and Prudential Securities use the *buy* rating as their highest rating. Yet you'll find that others, such as Alex. Brown, Morgan Stanley Dean Witter, and Pipper Jaffray, use *strong buy* as their highest rating. Each firm has several different ratings; some firms have more ratings than others. The big boys use the same number of ratings, which have the same meaning.

To become an able and successful man in any profession, three things are necessary: Nature, Study and Practice.

—Anonymous

Figure 4.1 Brokerage firms' equity ratings systems. Each firm's ratings are listed in descending order from the best to the worst. Some firms occasionally include long-term (L-T), intermediate-term (I-T), and near-term (N-T) classifications within their ratings systems. Investors should also be aware that firms are very cautious when downgrading a company. There is a school of thought that says that brokerage firms don't want to anger companies for fear of losing contacts or business

A. G. Edwards
Buy
Accumulate
Maintain position
Reduce
Sell

Alex. Brown
Strong buy
Buy
Neutral
Source of funds
Sell

Bear Stearns
Buy
Attractive
Neutral
Unattractive
Sell

Cowen & Co.
Strong buy
Buy
Hold
Underperform
Sell

CS First Boston
Strong buy
Buy
Sell

Donaldson, Lufkin & Jenrette (DLJ)
Recommended list
Buy
Market perform
Underperform

Everen Securities
Outperform
Market perform
Underperform

Goldman Sachs
Priority list
Recommended list

Goldman Sachs (Cont.)
Trading buy
Market outperform
Market perform
Market underperform

Gruntal
Strong buy
Outperform
Neutral
Underperform
Speculative

Hambrecht & Quist
Strong buy
Buy
Hold

Josephthal Lyon
Focus list buy
Buy

Josephthal Lyon (Cont.)
Hold
Sell

Lehman Brothers
Buy
Outperform
Neutral
Underperform
Sell

Merrill Lynch
Buy
Accumulate
Neutral
Reduce
Sell
No rating

Montgomery
Buy
Hold
Sell

Morgan Stanley Dean Witter
Strong buy

Figure 4.1   (Continued)

Morgan Stanley Dean Witter (Cont.)	Piper Jaffray (Cont.)	Salomon Smith Barney (Cont.)	Schroder Wertheim
Outperform	Market performer	Underperform	Outperform significantly
Neutral	Market under-performer	Avoid	Outperform
Underperform	Monitored	Note: Salomon Smith Barney attempts to incorporate risk measurement with the following further descriptions:	Perform-in-line
Nat West Securities			Underperform
Buy	**Prudential Securities**		Underperform significantly
Accumulate	Buy		
Trading buy	Hold		**SoundView Financial**
Underperform	Sell	Low risk—low volatility/high probability of strong earnings	Buy/buy
Hold			Hold/buy
Trading sell	**Raymond James**		Hold/hold
Sell	Buy		Sell
	Accumulate	Moderate risk—medium volatility / medium earnings potential	
Oppenheimer	Neutral		**Sutro & Co.**
Buy	Underperform		Strong buy
Outperform	Sell		Buy speculative
Market perform			Buy hold
Underperform	**Robertson, Stephens**	High risk—high volatility / low probability of strong earnings	Sell
Sell	Strong buy		
	Buy		**Wheat First Butcher Singer**
PaineWebber	Attractive	Speculative—risky on all counts	Buy
Buy	Market performer		Outperform
Attractive			Hold
Neutral	**Salomon Smith Barney**	Venture—for venture capital money only	Underperform
Unattractive	Buy		Sell
Sell	Outperform		
	Neutral		
Piper Jaffray			
Strong buy			
Buy			

I'd love to see a stock be raised from its lowest rating to its highest rating overnight; unfortunately, I haven't seen that happen yet. Typically, a firm will change its rating one day and then possibly again the next day. This is not as common with the upgrades, although you'll notice that a firm is quick to lower a rating several positions each day when bad news occurs. My understanding, after talking with many firms, is that they prefer to change their ratings on a company by raising or lowering the rating one grade at a time. This would make good sense, because investors have a tendency to overreact, even more so when a stock is downgraded.

The Impact of the Futures

The Standard & Poor's (S&P) futures are a key factor as to which direction the stock market will trade each day the market opens. Don't get the after-market-hour futures confused with such S&Ps as the S&P 500 and the S&P 100. To keep it simple, the after-hours futures are considered a commodity of cash buying or selling. The S&Ps seen on such television stock market reports as *CNBC and Bloomberg* are a composite of the S&P 500 stocks. The S&P 500 is a select group of stocks that create the S&P 500 index. The number you see is the total dollar amount of all 500 stocks. For example, if the S&P 500 is up 30, that means that after the individual gains and losses of all of those 500 stocks balance out, overall they're up $30. The same works for the downside: If the S&P 500 is down 30, the average of all 500 stocks equals a loss of $30.

Follow the futures as an indication of whether the market will open up or down. During market hours, you can continue to follow the S&Ps as a leading indicator to show which direction

---

Nothing is real unless it happens on television.

—Daniel J. Boorstein

the market should go. These indicators are very important in making decisions in the stock market; they have been proven to be an indication of the market direction. The market is very unpredictable, but you'll find that the market has a tendency to be up or down based on these futures.

Such indexes as the Dow 30 tend to follow the S&Ps in a more consistent pattern. The Dow 30 follows the direction of the S&Ps, with a value of about 7 to 8 points for every point that the S&Ps move. That is, if the S&Ps are up 8 at the time the market opens, the Dow will usually open and trade upward to about 56 to 64 points. This may be different on days when the market is very volatile.

The purpose of watching the futures at the market open is to allow you to make your decision whether to trade the up-grades or the downgrades. If the futures are trading in negative territory, you might want to consider making a bearish trade and playing the downgraded companies. The opposite is true if the futures are trading up; you might want to be bullish and fol-low the upgraded companies. When the futures are trading flat, it would be wise to stay on the sidelines until you're sure which direction the market is going to move. Now that you have an understanding of how the analysts can affect the stock, and the effects the S&Ps have on the market's direction, it's time to refer to the charts.

Charting for Profits

As the saying goes, "A picture is worth a thousand words." But in the stock market, a picture is worth thousands of dollars. You should never make a business decision regarding the stock

---

The most we can get out of life is its discipline for ourselves,
and its usefulness for others.

—Tyron Edwards

market unless you have properly analyzed a chart. The history of a chart is not only very important to understanding how a stock has performed in the past, it is also a good indication as to how the stock may perform in the future. I have found that the best charting service available is *TeleChart 2000,* offered by Worden Brothers, Inc. (1-800-776-4940). Without going into detail as to how valuable this system is, I would simply like to stress its importance by saying that it is a trading necessity. If you're not going to use the right tools, you shouldn't be in the business. This charting tool allows me to check several different indicators, such as the following:

- Balance of power
- Moving average
- Money stream
- Stochastics

These indicators are very important when trading the upgrades and downgrades. Another important indicator you want to look at is the recent picture of the stock's daily price movement. When playing the upgrades, you need to review the chart to assure yourself that the stock is not at its *resistance level* or, more important, that it is not trading at its 52-week high price. Stocks that are testing their resistance level (which is the point at which a stock tests a higher price level on an upward trend) may dip downward off the resistance level. If the stock does break through its resistance level, it may indicate a buying opportunity, because the stock may be in a position to split. I will make this trade only if I have researched the prior

---

The will to win is important, but the will to prepare is vital.

—Joe Paterno

split price and split date. On the other hand, if the stock does not break through its resistance level, you may see it dip downward, testing its previous support level. All of this information can be quickly accessed using TeleChart 2000.

Downgrades are no different than the upgrades when it comes to viewing the chart. Instead of looking at the stock's high point, you need to look at its low point, known as the *support level*. All stocks have a support level. It is important to locate the support level of a downgraded stock. The support level is the point where the stock will test its lows on a downward trend. If a stock breaks below its support level, it may test newer lows. When trading the downgrade (*shorting the stock* or *buying puts*), I look to see that the stock has room to run down several dollars before testing its support level. If the stock has recently broken through its support, I then look to see where its next support level is. This gives me an indication as to how low the stock can drop in value.

As mentioned, Worden Brothers' TeleChart is extremely valuable, as it provides many other indicators, such as the balance of power and the money stream, that can also be very helpful. The *balance of power* shows an indication as to whether the stock is being bought or sold. If you are trading an upgrade, you want to be sure that the stock is being bought more than sold. And if you are trading the downgrade, you want to make sure that the stock is being sold more than bought. Stocks move in certain directions—up if they are being bought and down if they are being sold.

The *money stream* indicates whether money has been going into or out of the stock. This is viewed by looking at two separate lines. The first is the 30-day line, and the second is the

---

Why is there so much month left at the end of the money?

—Anonymous

100-day line. The direction these two lines are pointing indicates whether the money is going into buying or selling that individual stock. If the 30- and 100-day moving averages are pointing upward, it can be a good indication for trading that upgraded stock. And if the 30- and 100-day moving averages are pointing downward, it can be a good indication for trading that individual downgraded stock.

Market Gaps

As you may know, *market makers* (also known as *specialists*) are the individuals who actually make the trade occur on the exchange floor. Market makers and specialists are those who maintain a bid and ask price in securities of their choice. These securities can be stock or options. When trading upgrades and downgrades, you must understand that any stock or option price can change prior to each market opening. You need to avoid getting sucked into their game. This is why you must know the previous closing price of the stock before making *any* trade. Again, this is easily done by referring to TeleChart. By checking the previous close price you'll be able to determine if a stock has gapped (changed in price prior to market open). Gapping can occur during market hours, but is not as likely to happen then as it is after market hours.

When a stock has gapped, you must decide whether the stock has the potential to trade higher or lower. If you're trading an upgrade, determine how far the stock can travel above and beyond the gapped opening price. If you're trading a downgrade, decide how far down the stock can travel below the

---

To win you have to risk loss.

—Jean-Claude Killy

gapped price. Market makers and specialists are in business for the same reason we are—to make money. If the stock or option has gapped considerably, I usually won't make the trade. Here's how to determine if the gap is considerable: If the stock has gapped up and you would be a seller based on the new trading price, then you shouldn't buy. Skip this stock and look at an alternative stock. If the alternative stock hasn't gapped out of range, then trade that one.

If a well-known stock has been upgraded or downgraded heavily and the gapping is too much to justify trading the stock, I'll look at other stocks in the same sector (type of business). When an analyst rates a stock up or down, you'll see a tendency for like businesses in that same sector to move in the direction as the up- or downgraded stock. For example, if Merck (MRK) is downgraded, I'll look at such companies as Pfizer (PFE), Bristol Meyer (BMY), Johnson & Johnson (JNJ), or others in that same type of business. The market, like the stocks, moves in the direction the money is going. So if Merck is downgraded and moves downward, you'll find that the others may follow. Investors have a tendency to invest or not to invest in certain sectors at certain times for certain reasons.

Market makers and specialists have a tendency to overinflate the gap in the direction of the market. If the market opens strong due to the S&Ps being up, the gapping of an upgraded stock may be higher due to the positive market direction. Make the opening trend your friend, and favor the stocks that can move with the direction of the market, not against the market direction. An upgrade has more potential to move up in an upward market, and a downgrade has more potential to move down in a downward market.

Man must be prepared for every event of life,
for there is nothing that is durable.

—Menander

A Bigger Bang for Your Money

Now that you have gathered your information and followed the outlined steps, you need to decide if you're going to trade the stock or the option. The deciding factor should be your *knowledge*—meaning that if you don't know how to properly trade options, then you're left with one choice: You need to trade the stock. When trading the stock, you have several advantages. One is that the stock opens for trading before the option does. Most options on almost all stocks roll out in a cycle—at certain strike prices, in certain months, and at certain times after the stock is already trading. In other words, when trading stock, you will be able to place the trade before the option trader. Second, when trading the stock, you will get a tick-for-tick movement in the stock—that is, for every dollar the stock moves, your investment will move the same dollar amount. The disadvantages of trading stocks are that the cost to buy the stock is a lot more than the cost to buy the option, and most brokerage firms don't allow you to *short* the stock, unless you have a minimum of about $200,000 in cash or securities in your account.

Shorting Stock

I'd like to explain the term *shorting stock,* so you will understand how someone else has the right to borrow your stock and make money on it without your knowledge. Understanding this is important, because this is the key to making money when you're trading a downgrade. Let's say you own 100 shares of XYZ company's stock and you've decided to hold the investment in your account until someday in the future. The stock that you have purchased is *not* locked up in a vault with your name on it. When you opened your brokerage account

---

All men's gain are the fruit of venturing.

—Herodotus

you agreed, if you read all that small print, that shorting your stock was acceptable.

Shorting a stock is also known as *selling short.* Selling short is the sale of a security (stock in this case) not owned by the seller at the time the trade is made. This technique is used for several reasons:

- To take advantage of a decline in the price of the stock
- To protect a profit in a long position
- To manipulate a stock value (done by specialists and market makers)

Example

I anticipate a decline in the price of XYZ stock and instruct my broker to sell short 100 shares of XYZ stock when the stock is trading at $50. The broker then loans me 100 shares of XYZ, using either their own inventory (shares in the margin account of another customer— *you*) or shares borrowed from another broker. I now have what is known as a *short position*—meaning, I do not own the 100 shares of XYZ stock. At some point, I must buy the stock to repay the lending broker or put the stock back into your account. If the market value of XYZ stock drops to $40, I can buy the stock for $4,000 ($40 per share × 100 shares = $4,000), then repay the lending broker, thus covering the short sale—and thereby claiming a profit of $1000 or $10 a share.

Now, let's recap the numbers on the short sale of the XYZ stock. The stock was trading at $50 per share. When I shorted 100 shares, I sold the 100 shares to some other investor, which netted my account $5,000 ($50 per share × 100 shares = $5,000).

Amateurs hope. Professionals work.

—Garson Kanin

The stock then dropped in value and is now trading at $40 per share. I buy the stock with the $5,000 that was put into my account and am left with the difference between the selling price and the actual buying price—$10 a share, or $1,000.

As you can see, this process amounts to selling a stock you never owned and keeping the profit. This is another reason why the emphasis of this book is on *selling* investments, not *holding* them. We business investors thank those people who buy and hold long-term investments, because they allow us to make money when the stocks are dropping in value. When trading a downgraded stock, you would make the trade the same way—sell the stock on the downgrade or bad news, and buy it back at your desired price (lower than what you sold the stock for).

Shorting stock is not risk free. If you sell the stock short thinking its value is going down, and the stock goes up, you have to make a decision as to when and at what price are you going to buy the stock. This means that if you short XYZ stock at $50 per share on 100 shares, and the stock then runs up to $53 per share, you now have to buy the stock for $53 per share—costing you $5,300. That's a loss of $3 per share, for a total loss of $300. Shorting stock can be very risky, which is why many brokers won't allow investors to do it. To me, shorting stock is no different from buying stock. When you buy a stock at a certain price, the value can drop just as fast as it can go up. If it drops, you are forced to sell the stock for a loss, or hold on to the stock with the hope that someday its value will go up so that you can sell it. Trading all boils down to having specialized knowledge and knowing how to make money as a business investor.

Each man has his own vocation. The talent is the call.

—Ralph Waldo Emerson

Putting Options to Work

If you have limited funds and can't afford to sell short, there is another way to invest. It is known as *trading the option*. With the right knowledge and the approval of your broker (which most brokers will grant, more so than approval to short stock) you can make money as the stock drops in value. This is called *buying puts*.

You buy a *call option* because you believe the stock is going to go up in value, so the opposite would be to buy a *put option* if you believe the stock is going to drop in value. The easiest way to remember this is: Pick *up* the phone to make a *call* (*call—up*) then *put down* the phone (*put—down*). When buying options, you'll have to make several decisions as to which option strike price and expiration month to buy. As the saying goes, it's better to be safe than it is to be sorry, so I like to buy the *in-the-money* options two months beyond the current month.

When buying put options, you might get confused at first, because put option strike prices are the same as the call option strike prices, but the terms *in the money* and *out of the money* are the opposite. When buying a *call* option, the term *in the money* applies when the stock is trading *above the strike price* of your option.

Example

A stock is trading at $53 per share, and you have purchased the $50 call strike price. Your call option is in the money by $3.

The exact opposite applies when buying a *put* option. Your option strike price is *above the stock price*. Say the stock is

---

They will conquer who believe they can.

—William Dryden

trading at $50 per share, and you have bought the next available strike price above the stock price—the $55 strike price. You have bought a put option that is in the money by $5. When buying a call or put option, you will always pay for the intrinsic value. Trading out-of-the-money put options is just as risky as trading out-of-the-money call options, so be sure the stock is going to travel in the right direction—otherwise, be quick to sell it for a loss. When you're wrong, it is better to sell for a small loss than to allow your option to expire worthless.

Taking Your Profits

Don't get greedy! Take small profits when they are available. A profit of $250 to $500 per day may not seem like a lot to many investors, but it adds up if you make just one profitable trade each trading day. There are 220 average trading days in a year—multiplied by $250, that is a total of $60,000 a year. That's a pretty nice income for most people.

The hardest time to tell: when to stop.

—Malcolm Forbes

chapter 5

stock splits

Fasten your seat belt, as we now go into the details of why companies split their stock. I will also explain many advantages of buying the stock and options of companies that do stock splits.

I have traveled throughout the country weekly asking students in my classes the same question, "Why do companies split their stock?" The two responses that I have heard over and over are the following:

- So the stock is more affordable.
- Because other companies in the same sector are splitting their stock, therefore allowing the company to stay in competition and take advantage of the momentum that the stock split creates.

Don't wait for your ship to come in; swim out to it.

—Anonymous

I absolutely agree that the stock becomes more afford-able, and companies usually do follow suit when other compa-nies in the same sector do a stock split. But let's not forget the main motivation behind the split. It is the executives and man-agers of the company (who control and own large blocks of the company's stock) who are behind the stock split.

Here is an example: At the time of this writing, one of my favorite stocks is Dell Computer (DELL), which has just com-pleted its seventh stock split since 1992. I recently read that Michael Dell (CEO of Dell Computer) has filed to sell 1,200,000 shares of stock after the recent 2-for-1 stock split. I don't know how many shares Dell personally owns, but I'm sure he has a fair amount. The current stock price value is $84 per share. Now, let's do the math:

$$1,200,000 \text{ shares} \times \$84 \text{ per share} = \$100,800,000$$

Wow! Now this would be considered a *block trade.* I must say that I respect Dell for waiting to sell his personal stock until after the split date to avoid causing a drop in the stock value due to his large sell order. A large sell order by any shareholder during the positive upward momentum could have driven the stock value down. (Also, keep in mind that as an employee of Dell Computer, there are restrictions on how often he can sell personal stock and on how much of it can be sold at a time.)

So, as mentioned, greed plays a roll in the decision making of a company stock split. But let's not discredit the company executives—this is a very wise business decision and it benefits the shareholders, as well. I'd like to keep it simple by saying

---

Purpose is the fuel that feeds success.

—Keith D. Harrell

that a company usually announces a stock split when the stock price has reached its all-time 52-week high or, for that matter, just an all-time high. This is not the only reason companies will announce stock splits, just the most popular reason.

Another reason might be that the company has been very profitable, driving the value of the stock higher. Or, the company could be in a position to acquire another publicly traded company whose stock value is higher. Following the acquisition, stock in the company being acquired will become stock in the company doing the acquiring. If the acquired company's stock value is $60, and the acquiring company's stock value is $30, it would make good business sense to have a 2-for-1 stock split, so the $30-stock investors don't gain an additional $30 in value. This is not done often and is not predictable; therefore, I do not invest anticipating this kind of event. I have also seen companies announce stock splits (for profit) before a projection of poor company earnings or other bad news is released. Always make sure to do your homework (research), and be sure a company is profitable.

If the company is going to do a 2-for-1 stock split, and you currently own 100 shares, you would receive 2 shares for every share you now own, or 200 shares. A 2-for-1 stock split is the most common. Some other common stock-split ratios are 3-for-1, 3-for-2, 4-for-1, 4-for-2, 5-for-1, and 5-for-2. If you are trading options, the strike price of the option splits at the same ratio as the stock.

Creative thinking will improve as we relate the new fact to the old and all facts to each other.

—John Dewey

Example

Status	Stock	Options
Before split	100 shares at $80	1 contract, $80 call option
After split	200 shares at $40	2 contracts, $40 call option

As you can see, the higher the ratio, the more opportunity there is for the investor. Also, companies may announce a *reverse stock split,* which is exactly how it sounds. You would receive the reverse number of shares. For example, a 1-for-5 reverse split would entitle the shareholder to 1 new share for every 5 existing shares. This kind of stock split is not very common and is usually done with spin-offs. (A *spin-off* occurs when a company spins off a division to form a separate company.)

More important, make sure the company has enough shares of stock in *float* to justify the ratio. The term *float* simply means the number of shares of stock that are available to the public for trading. This information is valuable to you, because a company can announce a stock split subject to the shareholders' approval, but can only make the actual agreement if the shareholders do approve and the stock becomes available.

It is also a good idea to check to see if the company has filed a 14A form with the Securities and Exchange Commission (SEC). The 14A filing is public information and informs the government whether the company has authorized a shareholders meeting, which is a good indication of an upcoming

---

A journey of a thousand miles must begin with a single step.

—Chinese proverb

stock split. You can acquire this valuable information either through your broker or through other news sources via the Internet.

There are also exceptions to the rule. For example, McDonald's (MCD) has obtained prior shareholder approval giving the company plenty of shares in float to do stock splits, provided the board members approved, but yet waited several years before agreeing to split the stock.

Boards do not have to disclose the date or the time that they will meet. It is important to get as much information as possible on a company if you are planning to invest. Usually, a split announcement is made right after the company has held a board meeting, but not always. Doing so limits the chances of the news being released to the market prematurely, which can run the stock value up before news of the split becomes public knowledge. Releasing this news to the market prematurely is considered *insider trading,* which is a violation of SEC regulations—a very serious offense. Many companies will elect not to release the information until a certain time or date. A good example of this is when a board meeting is held after hours, when the market is closed. You may see the announcement before the market opens, or even sometime during the following day.

I have seldom found a stock-split announcement that has a great potential of a short-term run up in the stock (or the option price), either before the market opens or after the market closes. This is due to the fact that the timing enables the market makers and specialists to inflate the price. This is otherwise known as a *gap up* in the stock price at the opening of the market.

Learn from the mistakes of others—you can't live long enough to make them all yourself.

—Martin Vanbee

The average investor can now trade the stock market after hours, but trading may still be limited. Certain investors are allowed to make certain trades based on different criteria. This is a major factor that creates increases or decreases in the stock or option value overnight, before the market opens.

I'd like to say that I don't believe in paying for *fluff* (a stock or option that is overpriced on the basis of rumor or news), but you may find that sometimes you should. There are several factors to take into consideration before paying for fluff:

- How much was the stock inflated?
- Can the stock travel higher?
- Is the market opening with strong momentum?

There are times that you may place a limit or market order higher than the asking price. This should be done only after you have acquired a certain amount of specialized knowledge using Strategy 2, played on the announcement of a stock split, as covered in Chapter 7. Market makers are quick to inflate a stock or option on an announcement, and they will be even quicker to take the premium back out as soon as the momentum of buying stops and the volatility slows down.

As a reminder, the difference between the bid and the ask price is the profit for the market makers; this is where their income is generated.

Example

Bid	Ask
23¼	23½

---

*It isn't as important to buy as cheap as possible
as it is to buy at the right time.*

—Jesse Livermore

Thus, a profit of 25 cents between what someone is willing to sell for and what another buyer is willing to pay.

The market makers are in business for a good reason—to make money. (You can think of the market makers as the *money makers,* also known as *thieves.*) They are very wise, you couldn't get out of bed early enough to outsmart them.

I speak of specialized knowledge, and I truly believe the market makers are extremely good at what they do and deserve much respect. They have great knowledge of the overall market and of how to control the prices and volatility of a security. I tend to agree that the option makers have a better advantage than the stock market makers, because the options roll out in cycles after the stock opens each morning. Options can sometimes open immediately, or they can open much later than the trading of the stock.

This allows the option and market makers the chance to adjust the premiums to their advantage, based on any news or the direction the stock seems to be trading at. As another reminder, not all options open on a delay. You may find that some options open almost immediately after the stock.

We need to discuss halting to understand how this can affect the price or option of any security. First of all, *halting a stock* means there is no trading taking place until the reopening has been given. This is not a set time delay; it varies from security to security. Normally, it is only a few minutes, but not always. Halting is common if a company has good or bad news that may dramatically affect the price of the stock. This is done during trading hours, which enables the market makers to adjust the prices accordingly. This is very common when a company announces a stock split during trading hours. Halting

---

*A billion here, a billion there, and pretty soon
you're talking about real money.*

—Everett M. Dirksen

the stock allows the market makers to adjust the prices up in consideration of the sudden increase in demand and the volatility of the stock due to the good news. When stocks are halted, so are the options.

You will find that sometimes the increase, or fluff, may be greater than you should pay. Be very careful—it is just as easy to lose money as it is to make money if you do not know what you are doing, or you get greedy.

Buying stocks or options after the security has just started trading is almost the same as buying at the opening of the market. You may find that you will lose money as the hype dies down. Be patient!

As you read on, you will see the value of making a lot of little profits in the stock market. In the next chapter, you will learn how to profit from various strategies, starting with the preannouncement of a stock split.

Wishes cost nothing unless you want them to come true.

—Frank Tyger

chapter 6

strategy 1: preannouncement

The first stock-split strategy I am going to discuss is the pre-announcement strategy. This comes into play when a company gets together for a shareholders meeting and decides whether to split the stock price. When the stock price splits, the price of the stock is more affordable, and more people tend to buy in, driving the price of the stock up.

You will see that this book includes many charts showing real profits, proving that more profits can be made with the buy-and-sell theory than with the buy-and-hold.

There are six stock-split strategies that can generate profits. Strategy 1, preannouncement, is probably the most profitable. I consider this strategy to be a guessing game only because

---

It is well to learn by the misfortunes of others.

—Publius Syrys

there are no guarantees that the company will announce a stock split, or even of when the split may occur. Understand that there is as much potential for making money as there is risk of losing it, so be very careful with the amount of money you invest.

I have spent thousands of hours, along with thousands of dollars, trying to keep the odds in my favor. I must say that the odds are always against you, even with the greatest knowledge and research. But, in analyzing my own trades, I have found that I am right more often than I am wrong. This is what makes this business profitable. And this is why I have focused on the preannouncement strategy, to help you better understand and learn from my experience—and my expenses. It is always nice when you can learn from someone who has tested the strategy over and over again and knows the right (and wrong) way to investing in preannouncements. It sure beats learning from the school of hard knocks.

When investing in the stock market, you should always follow the three-step process:

1. Gather information.
2. Analyze the information.
3. React, or decide *not* to react.

It is important to follow this process when investing in stock splits on preannouncement. Take time to gather information, analyze it, and react. If you decide not to react, then move on to the next deal. It's as simple as that.

A wise man should have money in his head, not in his heart.

—Jonathan Swift

Charting

Making money in the stock market is as easy as looking at a chart. You may have heard the saying, "A picture is worth a thousand words." Well, a chart is worth thousands of dollars. Charts show incredible information, starting with a picture of a potential stock split.

There are several different charting services available; I happen to use TeleChart 2000. The charts show the predictability of prior company stock splits, which, in turn, can indicate when they may do another split. Studying charts shows that companies usually do stock splits at their 52-week high price. The charts also show what kind of volume was traded and what the price increase was on the day of the announcement. What's exciting is that most companies that do stock splits return to their presplit stock price within 12 to 16 months, if not sooner. I find charts to be very helpful due to the fact that they show patterns, which make them useful predictive tools. Figures 6.1 to 6.3 show examples of such patterns.

Using Microsoft Corporation as an example, note that the chart in Figure 6.1 shows that the company is known for splitting its stock above the $130 range. You can see that the 52-week price high is exactly where the company announced a stock split. If the stock is at or near a 52-week price high, gather more information by referring to the 14A form to see what is on the company's agenda.

Now that you have a chart showing a 52-week price high, research the company a little further. Does this company have enough shares in float to do a stock split? *Float* means the number of company shares available for trading.

The market, like the Lord, helps those who help themselves.

—Warren Buffett

Figure 6.1 **Charts showing stock-split patterns: (a) Microsoft Corporation (MSFT), and (b) Dell Computer Corporation (DELL). (TC 2000 charts courtesy of Worden Brothers, Inc.)**

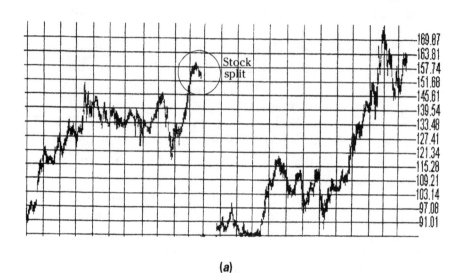

(a)

(b)

Figure 6.2 Charts showing stock-split patterns: (*a*) America Online, Inc. (AOL), and (*b*) Home Depot, Inc. (HD). (*TC 2000 charts courtesy of Worden Brothers, Inc.*)

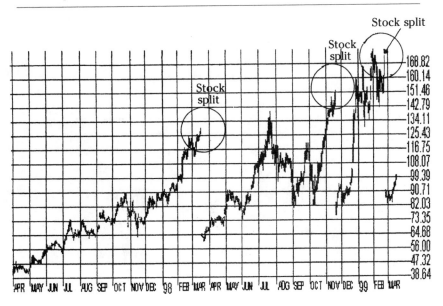

(*a*)

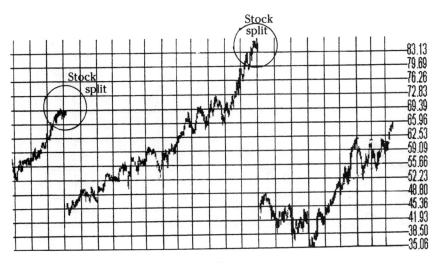

(*b*)

Figure 6.3   Charts showing stock-split patterns: (*a*) Lucent Technologies (LU), and (*b*) Pfizer, Inc. (PFE). (*TC 2000 charts courtesy of Worden Brothers, Inc.*)

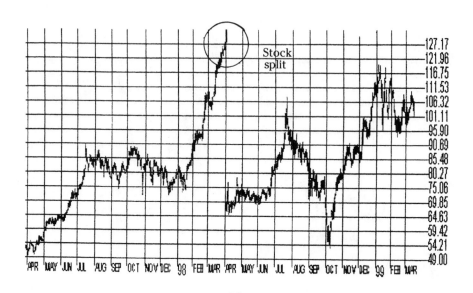

(*a*)

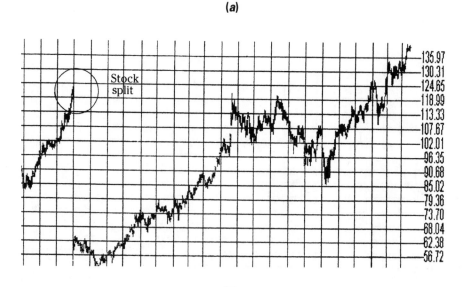

(*b*)

Find out what the last split ratio was (2-for-1, 3-for-1, or 3-for-2). Most companies will typically use the same ratio as the previous split. Once again, split ratios and other pertinent information can be found by using charts or Internet sites. If you find that the company has plenty of shares available for the proposed stock split, then go on to Step 2: Analyze the information.

If the company does not have enough shares in float, you might want to find out when the next shareholders meeting is and ask what is on the agenda for that meeting. Shareholders meetings are normally held in the town where the corporate office is located. As a shareholder, you have the privilege of attending the meeting, but you must have owned the stock before a certain date in order to qualify. Do not expect to purchase stock the day before the shareholders meeting with the hope of being able to attend. To minimize your research efforts, you could even go as far as to purchase one share in the company for the sole purpose of being kept up to date on all of the company information.

After purchasing stock in a company, you will receive a proxy. A *proxy* is a written power of attorney document given to shareholders of a corporation, authorizing a specific vote on their behalf at corporate meetings. Such proxies normally pertain to the election of the board of directors or to various resolutions submitted for the shareholders' approval.

Another way of obtaining the meeting minutes is to contact the company directly. Be sure you ask to speak to the public relations department. If you are unable to reach anyone in public relations, simply transfer back to the receptionist and ask questions. Oftentimes, you will be given the direct answers you are looking for without a runaround.

We should not ask who is the most learned,
but who is the best learned.

—Michel E. de Montaigne

The questions you will want to ask are when the shareholders meeting will be, and what the increase in shares will be. Also, ask if a board meeting is scheduled for the same day as the shareholders meeting. If not, then ask when the next board meeting will be held. (Board members decide whether to do a stock split and set the date when it will take place.) Companies are very hesitant to release information about their board meetings. If you can not get the information for the upcoming meeting, ask when the last two meetings were held. You may see a date pattern, which would be a good indication as to when the next meeting might be held.

If a company does not have enough shares in float but the shareholders agree to increase the number of shares, then the next step of research is to see if a 14A form has been filed with the Securities and Exchange Commission (SEC). You will find several types of 14A forms. I look for the two with the most detailed information, which are the PRE 14A and the DEF 14A. The PRE 14A form is a *preliminary proxy statement.* This statement provides official notification to designated classes of shareholders of matters that will be brought to a vote at the shareholders meeting. The DEF 14A form, known as the *final proxy filing,* officially provides designated classes of shareholders with all the current, updated information explaining what will be discussed and voted on at the shareholders meeting. This form is commonly referred to as a *proxy.*

The SEC requires that certain proxy statement information must be provided to shareholders before they vote by proxy on company matters. As you might expect, many companies provide Internet access to proxy information for shareholders. If the stock is at or near a 52-week high, gather more information by referring to the 14A form to see what is on the company's

---

The way to be nothing is to do nothing.

—Nathaniel Howe

agenda. Figure 6.4 shows the 14A filing for Home Depot. Note that item 4 shows an increase in authorized shares.

Another piece of important information that you will want to know is when the company will be releasing its next quarterly earnings. You may find that many companies elect to announce a stock split at the same time as they announce positive earnings. Companies may also issue an increase in dividends to the shareholders after releasing positive earnings. This would give you a double bang for your buck. It could give the stock more momentum and create more investor interest. We all like to invest in good companies, and if they have good earnings and a pattern of stock splits, that is just an added plus. The more good news they have, the more momentum the stock may have with upside potential, which could mean more money in your pocket.

Once you have contacted the company and received the information you need, ask for their toll-free number if you haven't already done so. Oftentimes you will be put on hold or will even have to call back several times, so let them pay for the call.

When you feel that you have satisfied your research requirements, be sure to keep all of your information on file with updates for the next split. After you have completed your research, you will need to decide whether to act. If you choose to act, you will need to decide whether to buy the stock or to purchase the option on the stock. Let's look at some examples of purchasing the stock versus purchasing call options.

Example

You purchase 1,000 shares of Home Depot stock at the current trading price of $68 a share:

1,000 shares $\times$ $68 per share = $68,000 investment

Too much of a good thing can be wonderful.

—Mae West

Figure 6.4   14A filed with the Securities and Exchange Commission by Home Depot

THE HOME DEPOT, INC.
2455 PACES FERRY ROAD
ATLANTA, GEORGIA 30339-4024

NOTICE OF ANNUAL MEETING OF STOCKHOLDERS
TO BE HELD MAY 27, 1998

NOTICE is hereby given that the Annual Meeting of Stockholders of The Home Depot, Inc., a Delaware corporation (the "Company" or "Home Depot"), will be held in accordance with its By-laws at the Cobb Galleria Centre, 2 Galleria Parkway, Atlanta, Georgia 30339, Wednesday, May 27, 1998, at 10:00 a.m. for the following purposes:

(1) To elect four (4) directors for terms ending with the 2001 Annual Meeting of Stockholders and until their successors are elected and qualified;

(2) To approve an amendment to the Company's Senior Officers' Bonus Pool Plan;

(3) To approve an Executive Officers' Bonus Plan;

(4) To consider and act upon a proposal to amend the Company's Certificate of Incorporation to increase the number of authorized shares of Common Stock from 1,000,000,000 to 2,500,000,000; and

(5) To conduct such other business, including consideration of two stockholder proposals, as may properly come before the meeting and any adjournments or postponements of the meeting.

The Common Stock of the Company should be represented as fully as possible at the Annual Meeting. Therefore, it will be appreciated if you will date, sign and return the enclosed proxy at your earliest convenience or vote your shares electronically via the telephone or the Internet. You may, of course, change or withdraw your proxy at any time prior to the voting at the meeting. However, returning the proxy in a timely manner will assure your representation at the Annual Meeting.

The Board of Directors has fixed the close of business on March 30, 1998, as the record date for the determination of holders of Common Stock of the Company entitled to notice of, and to vote at, the Annual Meeting and any adjournments thereof. A list of stockholders entitled to vote at the meeting will be available for inspection by any stockholder for any purpose germane to the meeting during ordinary business hours from May 18 through May 27, 1998, at the corporate offices of the Company and during the meeting.

By Order of the Board of Directors

Let's say the stock runs up $4 and is now trading at $72. Your investment is now worth $72,000. If you sell your stock at this price, your profit would be $4,000. Now, that's a good rate of return! Let's figure it out. The way you figure your rate of return is, by dividing the original invested dollar amount by the profits. This is known as the *cash-in/cash-out ratio.*

$$\frac{\$4,000 \text{ profit}}{\$68,000 \text{ investment}} = 5.9\% \text{ rate of return}$$

Before investing in options, you must first understand them. The definition of an *option* is the right (not the obligation) to buy or sell the stock at a certain price (known as the *strike price*) on or before a certain date (known as *expiration date*). Options are very risky and can expire worthless, having no value.

I like to purchase call options, but not with the intention of actually purchasing the stock. I buy call options merely for the profits. As the stock increases in value, the option also increases in value. A small movement in the stock can create a magnified movement in the option. Once I have made a profit, I sell the options and move on to the next investment. Remember, with options you have the right to buy or sell as long as you do so prior to your selected expiration date. When the stock moves up, so does the option. So, why not sell it for a profit?

Strike prices are set prices at which the investor agrees to buy or sell the stock. Strike prices are set by the options exchange clearing house. All strike prices are the same for all optionable companies. Options are not available for all compa-

---

No man can claim to be free unless he has a wage that permits him and his family to live in comfort.

—Sidney Hillman

nies. You will rarely find a company that offers options with a strike price below $5. The only time you might see this is after a company has done a stock split and the strike price has split below $5. Remember, not only does the stock price split; the option price also splits.

Strike prices are set as follows:

Stock Prices	Strike Prices
$5 to $25	$2.50 increments: $5.00, $7.50, $10.00, . . . $25.00
$25.00 to $200	$5 increments: $25, $30, $35, . . . $200
$200 and up	$10 increments: $200, $210, $220, . . .

Options are considered risky, mostly because they are a timed investment that have an expiration date. Options expire on the third Saturday of every month, depending on which month you buy. Technically, you are unable to trade on Saturday so simply put, options expire at the close of the market on the third Friday of every month.

When investing in options, you are able to buy options for future months, although there are exceptions depending on the cycle. Options over more than six months are known as long-term equity anticipation securities (LEAPS). Options are bought and sold in contracts only. One contract is equal to 100 shares. Ten contracts would equal 1,000 shares. By purchasing options you have the right to buy or sell the stock at the agreed strike price. The strategy is to buy or sell the option only after an increase in the option price.

In the business world, everyone is paid in two coins: cash and experience. Take the experience first; the cash will come later.

—Harold S. Geneen

When deciding which call option to purchase, there are several things to take into account. How should you decide which month to purchase the call option for? The first thing you should do is to be sure that the option won't expire until after the expected stock-split announcement. Remember, options are an investment in time as well as money, and if you are wrong about the date of the potential stock split, then your options may expire worthless, and you could lose your entire investment.

If time has passed and you're not sure whether the announcement will be made prior to your option expiration date, you could sell the call options and *roll out* to a further month. This simply means that you would buy the options for another month out to be sure they don't expire before the announcement.

Remember: Strategy 1 is a longer-term investment plan, so always buy plenty of time.

Time Value versus Intrinsic Value

Options have two parts. The first is called *time value*. Time value is the cost of your option's premium for the time remaining before its expiration date. The second part is called *intrinsic value*. Intrinsic value is what is considered to be the *equity* in your investment at that moment (the difference between your option strike price and the stock's current trading price).

Example

You purchase the June $65 call option for $5 a share (100 shares equals 1 contract).

To choose time is to save time.

—Francis Bacon

Stock price	$68
Strike price	− $65
Intrinsic value	$ 3
Call option cost	$5
Intrinsic value	− $3
Time value	$2

In this example, you would be paying $3 for intrinsic value (equity) and $2 for the time value (fluff). This option trade would meet the 50 percent rule.

50 Percent Rule

Many option investors have found several ways to determine what options to buy or sell. I like to use a simple formula known as the 50 percent rule. Basically, the 50 percent rule means you never pay more than 50 percent of your option premium for time, leaving the other 50 percent of the premium as equity.

Keep in mind that the time value of your option erodes each day, which can be detrimental, if the stock does not perform to your liking. Compare it to owning a home—you would rather have more equity in the home than outstanding debt, which ends up costing you a monthly premium, otherwise known as interest. Some options include so much time value simply because the market makers have added in the fluff (hype that the stock may have a run-up in value, due to positive news such as a potential stock split). When deciding which option to purchase, remember that the cheaper options aren't always the wisest investments.

As you will see in the next example, the further the option is *in the money* (more equity), the less you pay for time. The

---

Remember that time is money.

—Benjamin Franklin

strike prices from 65 to 70 are considered higher-risk investments. These investments have no equity value; therefore, the premium you are paying is 100 percent for time.

Example

The date is March 10—stock is trading at $64 a share.

Month	Strike Price	Premium	Amount Paid for Time
April	70c	N/A	0
April*	65c	2⅞	2⅞
April	60c	6	2
April	55c	10¼	1¼
May	70c	2⅜	2⅜
May*	65c	4⅜	3⅜
May	60c	6⅞	2⅞
May	55c	11	2

*Options closer to the stock price seem to be less desirable because of the time-value cost.

Keep in mind that the 50 percent rule will not work with *all* options. The stock's volatility and demand, along with several other things (like greedy market makers), can create a higher option value that doesn't meet the 50 percent rule.

Over time, you will gain a better understanding through experience and be able to know when it is right for you to make the trade and when it is better not to trade.

In the Money

In the Money is another term for intrinsic value. As mentioned earlier, intrinsic value is the equity in your investment. An

---

In all human affairs, the odds are always six to five against you.

—Damon Runyon

option is considered to be in the money if the option strike price is below the stock price.

Example

Stock price	$68
Strike price	− $65
In the money	$ 3

At the Money

At the money means exactly that—it is when the stock price and the strike price are the same dollar amount. When you are at the money, there is no Intrinsic value (equity).

Example

Stock price	$65
Strike price	− $65
At the money	$ 0

Out of the Money

Out of the money means that the stock price is less than the strike price.

Example

Stock price	$63
Strike price	− $65
Out of the money	− $ 2

This is known as being out of the money because there is no equity. With this type of option investing, you need to do your homework. This is a very risky play; all you are really paying for is time (time value). If the stock never reaches the strike

---

Nine-tenths of wisdom consists of being wise in time.

—Theodore Roosevelt

Figure 6.5   Confirmation slips of Home Depot options trade

You Bought
Trade Date 05/27/98 for Settlement on 05/28/98

Quantity	10	Price	3 3/8	Settlement Amount	
Description: CALL HOME DEPOT INC OPENING UNSOLICITED TRADE		AT 75 EXPIRES 07-18-1998		Principal Commission H/P/I Trans Fee Net Amount	$3,375.00 76.65 2.35 7.00 **$3,461.00** **BOUGHT**

You Sold
Trade Date 05/28/98 for Settlement on 05/29/98

Quantity	10	Price	4 3/4	Settlement Amount	
Description: CALL HOME DEPOT INC CLOSING UNSOLICITED TRADE		AT 75 EXPIRES 07-18-1998		Principal Commission S.E.C. Fee H/P/I Trans Fee Net Amount	$4,750.00 85.24 0.16 2.35 7.00 **$4,655.25** **SOLD**

PROFIT $ 1,194.25

price, the option will not gain very much intrinsic value (equity). As the option gets closer to the date of expiration, the time value begins to melt like an ice cube. Remember, you get what you pay for. With less expense, there is always more risk involved. Out-of-the-money options are less expensive not only because of the risk that the stock will fail to go up in value

---

The future belongs to those who believe
in the beauty of their dreams.

—Eleanor Roosevelt

Figure 6.6   Confirmation slips of Excite options trade

You Bought
Trade Date 06/16/98 for Settlement on 06/17/98

Quantity 5	Price 4 1/2	Settlement Amount
Description: CALL EXCITE INC AT 70 EXPIRES 07-18-1998 OPENING UNSOLICITED TRADE		Principal $2,250.00 Commission 50.14 HI/P/I 2.35 Trans Fee 3.50 Net Amount **$2,305.99** **BOUGHT** Security No. 8L944 Symbol CKQBJU70

You Sold
Trade Date 06/18/98 for Settlement on 06/19/98

Quantity 5	Price 9 1/2	Settlement Amount
Description: CALL EXCITE INC AT 70 EXPIRES 07-18-1998 CLOSING UNSOLICITED TRADE		Principal $4,750.00 Commission 67.51 S.E.C. Fee 0.16 HI/P/I 2.35 Trans Fee 3.50 Net Amount **$4,676.48** **SOLD** **PROFIT $ 2,370.49** Security No. 8L944 Symbol CKQBJU70

Mediocre men often have the most acquired knowledge.

—Claude Bernard

Figure 6.7   Confirmation slips of Immunex options trade

Stocks and Bonds   SIPC
CONFIRMATION

MEMBER NATIONAL ASSOCIATION OF SECURITIES DEALERS, INC. & CHICAGO STOCK EXCHANGE

ORIGINATOR	ACCOUNT NUMBER	TRANS. NO.	TR.	*CAP	SETT.	*AA	TRADE DATE	SETTLEMENT DATE	ENTRY DATE
C	001	054-2907	087	3-D		4	02/23/99	02/24/99	

TAX I.D. NO.		CONTRA PARTY		SYMBOL		SPECIAL DELIVERY INSTRUCTIONS
				IUQDJ.		

0
FROZEN-051999

ACCOUNT OF:
OR SPECIAL
DISPOSITION

BOUGHT

	QUANTITY	CUSIP NUMBER	SECURITY DESCRIPTION	NET AMOUNT
YOU BOT	10	4525289DJ	CALL-IMMUNEX CORP APR 150 04/17/1999	14,447.25

OPENING TRANSACTION   UNSOLICITED ORDER

PRICE	PRINCIPAL AMOUNT	INTEREST	* COMMISSION	TAX OR FCF	MISC.	S.E.C. FEE	A-E
14-3/8	14375.00		68.75			3.50	D R1

Stocks and Bonds   SIPC
CONFIRMATION

MEMBER NATIONAL ASSOCIATION OF SECURITIES DEALERS, INC. & CHICAGO STOCK EXCHANGE

ORIGINATOR	ACCOUNT NUMBER	TRANS. NO.	TR.	*CAP	SETT.	*AA	TRADE DATE	SETTLEMENT DATE	ENTRY DATE
C	001	054-2909	087	3-D		J	02/23/99	02/24/99	

TAX I.D. NO.		CONTRA PARTY		SYMBOL		SPECIAL DELIVERY INSTRUCTIONS
				IUQDJ.		

0
FROZEN-051999

ACCOUNT OF:
OR SPECIAL
DISPOSITION

SOLD

	QUANTITY	CUSIP NUMBER	SECURITY DESCRIPTION	NET AMOUNT
YOU SLD	10	4525289DJ	CALL-IMMUNEX CORP APR 150 04/17/1999	16,668.44

CLOSING TRANSACTION   UNSOLICITED ORDER   **PROFIT $2,221.19**

PRICE	PRINCIPAL AMOUNT	INTEREST	* COMMISSION	TAX OR FCF	MISC.	S.E.C. FEE	A-E
16 3/4	16750.00		77.50		3.50	.56	R R1

A nickel ain't worth a dime any more.

—Yogi Berra

Figure 6.8   Confirmation slips of Sun Microsystems options trade

Stocks and Bonds   **SiPC**

CONFIRMATION

MEMBER NATIONAL ASSOCIATION OF SECURITIES DEALERS, INC. & CHICAGO STOCK EXCHANGE

ORIGINATOR	ACCOUNT NUMBER	TRANS. NO.	TR.	*CAP	SETT.	*A/I	TRADE DATE	SETTLEMENT DATE	ENTRY DATE
C 001		334-0217	087	3-D		4	11/30/98	12/01/98	

TAX I.D. NO.   CONTRA PARTY   SYMBOL   SPECIAL DELIVERY INSTRUCTIONS.

SUQAO.

0

ACCOUNT OF:
OR SPECIAL
DISPOSITION

BOUGHT

	QUANTITY	CUSIP NUMBER	SECURITY DESCRIPTION	NET AMOUNT
YOU BOT	10	8668109A0	CALL-SUN MICROSYSTEM IN JAN 75 01/16/1999	6,202.50

OPENING TRANSACTION   UNSOLICITED ORDER

PRICE	PRINCIPAL AMOUNT	INTEREST	*COMMISSION	TAX OR PCF	MISC.	S.E.C. FEE	A/I
6 1/8	6125.00		74.00		3.50		D R1

Stocks and Bonds   **SiPC**

CONFIRMATION

MEMBER NATIONAL ASSOCIATION OF SECURITIES DEALERS, INC. & CHICAGO STOCK EXCHANGE

ORIGINATOR	ACCOUNT NUMBER	TRANS. NO.	TR.	*CAP	SETT.	*A/I	TRADE DATE	SETTLEMENT DATE	ENTRY DATE
C 001		335-2770	087	3-D		J	12/01/98	12/02/98	

TAX I.D. NO.   CONTRA PARTY   SYMBOL   SPECIAL DELIVERY INSTRUCTIONS.

SUQAO.

0

ACCOUNT OF:
OR SPECIAL
DISPOSITION

SOLD

	QUANTITY	CUSIP NUMBER	SECURITY DESCRIPTION	NET AMOUNT
YOU SLD	10	8668109A0	CALL-SUN MICROSYSTEM IN JAN 75 01/16/1999	8,527.46

PROFIT $ 2,324.96

CLOSING TRANSACTION   UNSOLICITED ORDER

PRICE	PRINCIPAL AMOUNT	INTEREST	*COMMISSION	TAX OR PCF	MISC.	S.E.C. FEE	A/I
8 5/8	8625.00		93.75		3.50	.29	R R1

Abstinence from enjoyment is the only capital.

—Thomas Brassey

before the expiration date, but also because there has been no investment for equity.

The bottom line is, the more time you have, the better the odds are that you will have plenty of time remaining in the option after the announcement of the stock split. This enables the buyer of your options to exercise the option to buy the stock, as it was not your intention to buy the stock but to sell the option for a profit.

Now that you have a better understanding of options, let's look at an actual trade to show the real power of gathering knowledge and doing the proper homework. As this chapter was being written, I purchased call options for Home Depot the day before the company announced a stock split, and then sold them the following day (the day of the announcement). Earlier in this chapter I gave an example of purchasing the stock; now I am going to show an example of buying the call options.

Example

I purchased July call options on 10 contracts (1,000 shares) of Home Depot.

	Bid	*Ask*
Stock price	67¾ ×	68
July $75 call option	3 ×	3⅜ (or $3.00 × $3.37)

10 contracts at $3.37 = $3,370.00

After I purchased the July $75 call options for 3⅜ ($3.37), the stock price went up to $72 and I sold my options for 4¾ ($4.75). Now, let's complete the trade by figuring out the rate of return:

America is too great for small dreams.

—Ronald Regan

$$\frac{\text{Cash in}}{\text{Cash out}} = \frac{\$1,375 \text{ profit}}{\$3,375 \text{ investment}}$$

$$= 40.7\% \text{ rate of return (minus commissions)}$$

To prove my point, Figures 6.5 to 6.8 show confirmation slips of trades of Home Depot, Excite, Immunex, and Sun Microsystems (excluding personal information, of course). These trades took one and two days to generate profits. Now you can understand why it is a wise choice to play stock options. Now, go back to the beginning of the chapter and compare the difference between trading the stock and trading the option.

---

*The will to win is worthless if you do not have the will
to prepare.*

—Thand Yost

chapter 7

strategy 2: announcement

The announcement stock-split strategy is one of my personal favorites, due to its greater and faster return. However, along with the greater and faster return comes the infamous threat of risk. *Risk* is a word that will always be in our vocabulary as long as we are investing in the stock market. My advice to you is to accept the word, but limit the risk—Although when there is more risk, there are usually more rewards.

Strategy 2 is to be played only on the announcement date. This is a fast play and could last only a few minutes. If you don't have the capability to react immediately, you could end up losing a lot of money.

There are many sources available that will provide you

To be prepared is half the victory.

—Miguel Cervantes

with news of the announcement. I use www.splittrader.com. Services of this nature are very expensive, but the expeditious information they offer makes them well worth it. The importance of this service is that how quickly you receive the news of the announcement determines your profit. One good trade made from the news from Splittrader will pay for an entire year's worth of service.

After properly following all of the steps for a preannouncement trade, you should have already anticipated the day when the announcement of the split may be released to the public. I suggest that you give your brokers the list of potential stock splits so they will be ready to respond quickly.

If you have done the proper research, you will have been able to determine what day and time the shareholders meeting will be held, and you should have a better idea of whether the announcement will be made during market hours. It is best to either purchase call options during market-hour announcements or wait for the hype to settle back down and then reconsider. Do not chase any running stock or option. (Remember to set your limits.)

As mentioned, this is a fast play and time is of the essence, so you need to be sure that your trade has been confirmed. Online trading should be used cautiously when playing the stock split due to the fact that you may not get your order filled or receive a confirmation fast enough. Timing is very important.

There are two types of fast trades. When I place an order through my broker, the broker immediately picks up the other phone (while keeping me on the line), calls the market maker on the exchange floor directly, and places the order while keeping both myself and the exchange on the line until my order is filled. The broker receives verbal confirmation from the floor

---

To think is to act.

—Ralph Waldo Emerson

and relays the information to me within seconds. The other type of fast trade is when the brokerage firm is able to process my trades electronically through the computer within 10 seconds. The electronic order is picked up immediately by a market maker on the exchange floor and then transferred to the pit (area of exchange where the stocks or options are traded). These orders are transferred to the pit in two ways:

- One trader uses hand signals to relay the order to another trader in the pit.
- One trader *runs* the order over to another trader in the pit.

If you ever get an opportunity to visit an exchange, you will see that they are very serious about their running. Some exchanges even go so far as to post "No Walking Allowed" signs.

Timing makes all the difference in the execution of an order. I'm sharing this information with you to help you become the best trader you can possibly be, and also to help you understand how important it is to have the right tools to make your business successful.

As Benjamin Franklin once said, "Time is money." Make sure the brokerage firm you use to place your trades is going to give you the best possible service in the quickest amount of time. In my opinion, some firms need to either get with the system or get out of the business. If you're trading options, then you need to find the right brokerage firm.

Let's take a moment to discuss the different options exchanges. Options can be traded through different exchanges. What that means to you is that another exchange could be offering a better price for the option that you are looking to buy or

---

Luck sometimes visits a fool, but never sits down with him.

—German proverb

sell. Some options may only be offered at a certain exchange, leaving you no choice. Make sure your broker checks to be certain that you are getting the most for your money.

If you are buying options, why not pay the lower asking price? The same goes when you decide to sell. I justify this by reasoning that it gets the brokers to work for their commissions. If you add up ⅛ of a point on each trade, it begins to add up. My broker does a good job, and will get me a better fill price on my order 90 percent of the time.

Now you are ready and awaiting the moment of truth. The announcement comes across the screen (or whatever your source of information) that Home Depot (HD) has just announced a 2-for-1 stock split. How will you react? You should already know what strike price and month you want to buy the option for. If there is less than two weeks left before the date of expiration, then I would usually look at the next month out and sometimes even further. I say *usually* because if the option for that month is very inexpensive, then I might consider buying in for a quick 50-cent-per-share profit. With this quick, short-term play, I would buy no less than 10 contracts; otherwise, the commissions will eat up your profits.

Example

10 contracts = 1,000 shares

Shares	1,000
Profit per share	× $ 0.50
Gross profit	$500.00
Commissions	− $ 90.00
Net profit	$410.00

All the mistakes I ever made were when
I wanted to say "No" and said "Yes."

—Moss Hart

The deeper in the money you buy, the safer you are. If the stock split was anticipated by many investors, these options may be very expensive. I look at the strike price closest to the stock price, and if the price is reasonable, I will buy the in-the-money calls. I may even buy the out-of-the-money calls, but remember, they are riskier. Based on my previous trades, I have noticed that if the stock has been trading above that strike price in the past, then the stock may have potential to continue to climb higher. Obviously, the out-of-the-money calls are cheaper because they will end up worthless if the stock doesn't rally up. The option premium will quickly be taken out as the expiration date approaches—the ice cube melts!

I have practiced this strategy over and over, and I am not afraid to take chances based on the research I have done on a company's split history. If the company has no split history, it tells me to be very cautious and triggers me to buy only in-the-money calls with more time.

If you have done the proper research in Strategy 1, you would have bought call options with plenty of time, thus taking you beyond the announcement date. Strategy 1 has now become a very profitable trade, so you may choose to be conservative, like me, and buy fewer contracts in the money.

During the same call to my broker at the time of the announcement, I will also place an order to sell the call options that I had previously purchased under Strategy 1. If you were already in before the announcement, you may come out with a nice profit. This is a great time to sell and receive the fluff premium. You may also choose to use a *trailing stop loss*. A trailing stop loss is no more than moving your stop loss *up* to maximize your profits as the stock runs up *higher.*

Every accomplishment starts with the decision to try.

—Anonymous

Example

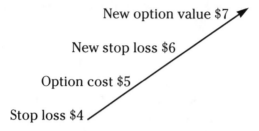

New option value $7

New stop loss $6

Option cost $5

Stop loss $4

It is wise to move your stop loss up as the stock moves up, so that if the option turns around and moves down, you will still sell your option for a profit.

When you have maximized your investment, it is time to sell, sell, sell. This is a great time to maximize your return, as everyone is wanting to buy, and you are selling for *top dollar.* If you choose not to sell, you may see the premium depreciate within 15 minutes, surely within an hour.

Figures 7.1 and 7.2 show option quotes provided by Bloomberg. You will note that the option price has increased more than that of the stock, and the times indicate that I have chosen to sell my options the same day.

Let's go back to the announcement play—when you call your broker, always remember to ask for the open interest. The open interest represents how many trades have been done on that particular option. I like to buy options that have the most open interest—meaning that the option has a lot of volatility and is being traded more often than the other options. There have been times when I haven't done the research on a company announcing a stock split, and I have reacted by quickly calling my broker simply because I have received the news over my pager. I always start by asking what the open interest

---

Ain't no chances if you don't take it.

—Guy Clark

Figure 7.1 Charts showing buy and sell points for Theragenics options trade. (*Bloomberg terminal chart courtesy of Bloomberg L.P.*)

THRX US $ ↓ 66³₈ +2⁵₈ Q 1s   Q ↑66¹₄/66⁷₁₆ Q 2x1   Equity OCM
At 11:08 Vol 289,400 Op 64¹₄ Q Hi 66¹₂ Q Lo 63⁷₈ Q ValTrd 18875112
Option Custom Monitor   Hit OCDF ▓▓ to Change Column Choices.
Calls on THERAGENICS CORP   Puts on THERAGENICS CORP 11:08

						THRX US						
2 m	**3 m**	**22**	**23**	**5 m**	**10 m**	Price 66³₈	**2 m**	**3 m**	**22**	**23**	**5 m**	**10 m**
Current BID PRICE	Current ASK PRICE	Current IMPLD VOLAT. BID	Current IMPLD VOLAT. ASK	Current LAST TRADE	Current 1-DAY NET CHANGE	+2⁵₈	Current BID PRICE	Current ASK PRICE	Current IMPLD VOLAT. BID	Current IMPLD VOLAT. ASK	Current LAST TRADE	Current 1-DAY NET CHANGE
66¹₄	66⁷₁₆			66³₈	+2⁵₈	XQ Mar98	66¹₄	66⁷₁₆			66³₈	+2⁵₈
40⁷₈	41¹₂			20⁵₈	unch	1) 25 15)			³₁₆		426.69	⁵₈ unch
35⁷₈	36¹₂			34	unch	2) 30 16)			¹₁₆		300.52	⁷₁₆ unch
30⁷₈	31¹₂			25	unch	3) 35 17)			³₁₆		290.92	¹₄ unch
25⁷₈	26¹₂			23³₈	unch	4) 40 18)			³₁₆		237.58	¹₈ unch
20⁷₈	21¹₂			19¹₄	unch	5) 45 19)			³₁₆		188.85	³₁₆ unch
15⁷₈	16¹₂			13⁷₈	unch	6) 50 20)			³₁₆		144.63	³₁₆ unch
11	11⁵₈		88.92	10	+¹₂	7) 55 21)			³₁₆		103.54	³₁₆ unch
6¹₄	6³₄			5⁷₈	+1¹₈	8) 60 22)			³₁₆		63.77	1³₁₆ unch
2¹₄	(2⁹₁₆) **BOUGHT**			2¹₈	+¹³₁₆	9) 65 23)	0⁷₈	1¹₈	50.30	56.71		¹⁵₁₆ -1¹₈
						XQ Apr98						
16⁵₈	17¹₄		71.70	15	unch	10) 50 24)	¹₄	⁷₁₆	60.40	68.66		¹₂ unch
12¹₈	12³₄	48.19	64.81	7⁵₈	unch	11) 55 25)	0³₄	1	58.81	64.80		1¹₄ unch
9⅛	9⁵₈	66.09	73.64	8¹₄	+³₄	12) 60 26)	2	2⁵₁₆	60.48	65.24		2⁵₈ unch
5⁷₈	6³₈	62.01	65.24	6³₈	+2³₈	13) 65 27)	4¹₈	4¹₂	62.26	67.07		4¹₂ unch
3⁵₈	4	57.92	62.70	3³₄	+1³₈	14) 70 28)	6³₄	7¹₄	61.44	67.83		7³₄ unch

THRX US $ ↓ 68⁹₁₆ +4¹³₁₆ Q ↑68³₈/68⁹₁₆ Q 5x1   Equity OCM
At 11:51 Vol 481,900 Op 64¹₄ Q Hi 69¹₄ Q Lo 63⁷₈ Q ValTrd 31899530
Option Custom Monitor   Hit OCDF ▓▓ to Change Column Choices.
Calls on THERAGENICS CORP   Puts on THERAGENICS CORP

						THRX US						
2 m	**3 m**	**22**	**23**	**5 m**	**10 m**	Price 68.56	**2 m**	**3 m**	**22**	**23**	**5 m**	**10 m**
Current BID PRICE	Current ASK PRICE	Current IMPLD VOLAT. BID	Current IMPLD VOLAT. ASK	Current LAST TRADE	Current 1-DAY NET CHANGE		Current BID PRICE	Current ASK PRICE	Current IMPLD VOLAT. BID	Current IMPLD VOLAT. ASK	Current LAST TRADE	Current 1-DAY NET CHANGE
68³₈	68⁹₁₆			68⁵₁₆	+4¹₃₆	XQ Mar98	68³₈	68⁹₁₆			68⁹₁₆	+4¹₃₆
43	44		500.00	20⁵₈	unch	1) 25 15)			¹₄		458.41	⁵₈ unch
38	39		420.24	34	unch	2) 30 16)			¹₁₆		310.32	⁷₁₆ unch
33	34		349.79	25	unch	3) 35 17)			¹₄		319.24	¹₄ unch
28	29		288.66	23³₈	unch	4) 40 18)			¹₄		262.07	¹₈ unch
23	24		234.30	19¹₄	unch	5) 45 19)			¹₄		211.85	¹₄ unch
18¹₈	18⁷₈		170.23	13⁷₈	unch	6) 50 20)			¹₄		167.10	³₁₆ unch
13¹₄	14		138.07	14	+4¹₂	7) 55 21)			¹₄		124.25	³₁₆ unch
8³₈	8⁷₈	**SOLD**		8³₄	+4	8) 60 22)			¹₄		84.03	1³₁₆ unch
(4¹₄)	4⁵₈			4⁷₈	+3³₁₆	9) 65 23)	1¹₁₆	1⁵₁₆	63.81	74.10		³₄ -1⁵₈
						XQ Apr98						
18³₄	19¹₂		83.79	15	unch	10) 50 24)	¹₈	³₈	57.61	71.45		¹₂ unch
14¹₈	14⁷₈	51.56	72.91	7⁵₈	unch	11) 55 25)	⁵₈	⁷₈	61.93	68.34		1¹₄ unch

Figure 7.2   Charts showing buy and sell points for BMC Software options trade. (*Bloomberg terminal chart courtesy of Bloomberg L.P.*)

BMCS US $ ↑ 96¹₂ +1   Q 10s   Q 196¹₆/96⁵₈ Q 5x10   Equity OCM
→ At 11:59 Vol 731.300 Op 95¹₄ Q Hi 96⁵₈ Q Lo 94¹₂ Q ValTrd 69604560
Option Custom Monitor Hit OCDF ▣ to Change Column Choices.
Calls on BMC SOFTWARE INC   **Puts** on BMC SOFTWARE INC

BID PRICE	ASK PRICE	Current IMPLD VOLAT. BID	Current IMPLD VOLAT. ASK	Current LAST TRADE	Current 1-DAY NET CHANGE	BMCS US Price 96¹₂ +1	BID PRICE	ASK PRICE	Current IMPLD VOLAT. BID	Current IMPLD VOLAT. ASK	Current - LAST TRADE	Current 1-DAY NET CHANGE
96³₁₆	96⁵₈			96¹₂	+1	BCQMay98	96³₁₆	96⁵₈			96¹₂	+1
41	42	126.02	24¹₂	unch		1) 55 15)		¹₁₆			108.89	¹₈ unch
36¹₈	37	108.23	22¹₄	unch		2) 60 16)		³₁₆			93.68	³₈ unch
31¹₈	32¹₈	91.93	29¹₄	unch		3) 65 17)		³₁₆			79.72	¹₂ unch
26¹₄	27¹₈	81.24	12¹₂	unch		4) 70 18)		³₁₆			66.81	¹₂ unch
21¹₄	22¹₈	70.18	21³₈	+1¹₄		5) 75 19)		³₁₆			54.30	¹₈ unch
16³₈	17	52.10	16⁷₈	unch		6) 80 20)	¹₁₆	³₁₆	35.08	42.33	⁵₁₆ unch
11³₄	12¹₂	31.37	45.88	11	-³₈	7) 85 21)	³₈	0⁹₁₆	36.22	40.63	¹¹₁₆ unch
7³₄	8¹₈	35.74	42.32	7¹₈	+¹₈	8) 90 22)	1¹₄	1⁷₁₆	38.12	40.58	1¹³₁₆ +⁵₁₆
4⁵₈	(4⁵₈)	**BOUGHT**		4³₈	+¹₈	9) 95 23)	3	3¹₄	37.46	39.98	3⁵₈ +¹₈
2³₈	2⁹₁₆	37.27	39.18		2⁹₁₆	10) 100 24)	5⁵₈	6	37.81	41.68	6³₈
						BCQJun98						
13¹₂	14¹₄	39.34	44.95			11) 85 25)	1³₄	1¹¹₁₆	40.58	42.23	2¹₆ +¹₈
10¹₈	10¹₂	40.31	43.16	10¹₂		12) 90 26)	3¹₈	3³₈	40.09	41.97	
7¹₄	7¹₂	40.18	42.64	6⁷₈	+¹₈	13) 95 27)	5¹₄	5⁵₈	40.09	42.54	5⁵₈ unch
5	5¹₈	40.27	41.87			14) 100 28)	7⁷₈	8¹₄	40.17	42.59	

BMCS US $ ↑ 98¹₄ +2³₄ Q 4s   Q ↑98/98¹₄   Q 13x10   Equity OCM
→ At 12:10 Vol 1,258,700 Op 95¹₄ Q Hi 98⁵₈ Q Lo 94¹₂ Q ValTrd 120.990m
Option Custom Monitor Hit OCDF ▣ to Change Column Choices.
Calls on BMC SOFTWARE INC   **Puts** on BMC SOFTWARE INC 12:10

BID PRICE	ASK PRICE	Current IMPLD VOLAT. BID	Current IMPLD VOLAT. ASK	Current LAST TRADE	Current 1-DAY NET CHANGE	BMCS US Price 98¹₄ +2³₄	BID PRICE	ASK PRICE	Current IMPLD VOLAT. BID	Current IMPLD VOLAT. ASK	Current LAST TRADE	Current 1-DAY NET CHANGE
98	98¹₄			98¹₄	+2³₄	BCQMay98	98	98¹₄			98¹₄	+2³₄
43	44	149.41	24¹₂	unch		1) 55 15)		³₁₆			111.67	¹₈ unch
38¹₈	39	129.98	22¹₄	unch		2) 60 16)		³₁₆			96.47	³₈ unch
33¹₈	34	112.17	29¹₄	unch		3) 65 17)		³₁₆			82.51	¹₂ unch
28¹₈	29¹₈	59.66	98.23	12¹₂	unch	4) 70 18)		³₁₆			69.61	¹₂ unch
23¹₄	24¹₄	46.92	85.27	21³₈	+1¹₄	5) 75 19)	¹₁₆	³₁₆	47.95	57.37	¹₈ unch
18¹₂	19¹₈	49.56	68.88	16⁷₈	unch	6) 80 20)	¹₄	³₈	48.30	52.55	⁵₁₆ unch
14¹₈	14³₄	51.09	63.56	13⁷₈	+2¹₂	7) 85 21)	³₄	¹⁵₁₆	48.29	51.90	¹¹₁₆ unch
10¹₈	10⁷₈	51.37	57.51	10	+3	8) 90 22)	1³₄	2	48.83	52.09	1¹³₁₆ +⁵₁₆
(7)	7	**SOLD** .41	7¹₄	+3		9) 95 23)	3³₈	3⁵₈	48.23	50.83	3¹₄ -¹₄
4¹₂	4¹₂	51.42	52.63	4³₈		10) 100 24)	5⁷₈	6¹₄	47.80	51.47	5³₈
						BCQJun98						
15⁵₈	16³₈	45.36	51.92			11) 85 25)	1¹⁵₁₆	2¹₁₆	44.15	45.41	2¹₆ +¹₈
12¹₈	12³₄	45.28	49.98	10¹₂		12) 90 26)	3³₈	3⁵₈	43.66	44.60	3³₈

is—there have often been times when *I* was the open interest. So, my experience teaches that you should be safe and buy call options on the most active options—otherwise you might be the *only* buyer.

Breaking News

As I sit here writing this chapter, I receive a stock-split announcement over my pager. I quickly call my broker. The ticker symbol is EFS—Enhance Group—and the company has just announced a 2-for-1 stock split—options available—last trade 65¼, up ¾ on the day. I haven't done any research on this company, so my first request to my broker is to check the open interest on the June and July $65 and $70 call options. There have been no trades on these options. Next I check what the daily volume for the stock has been today. The volume is 77,300 shares. Once again, the volume is like the open interest—very low. The market has been open for three hours, so this would be considered low volume for the day.

As I research the company further, I find that the volume over the past 3 days has been 57,100, 57,500, and 27,500. This is very low volume for a stock that is announcing a stock split. I like to see a consistent volume of at least 100,000 shares traded daily—and, obviously, the more shares traded the better. In fact, 300,000 shares traded daily is usually a good figure to go by. One thing that does come to my attention is that EFS is an insurance company, like Allstate Insurance (ALL), which just announced a stock split last week. This news triggers me to look at other companies in this same sector. Once again, timing is everything. As I write about lack of volume, the EFS split announcement happens to be a perfect example of a stock split

---

My father dealt in stocks and shares and my mother also had a lot of time on her hands.

—Hermione Gingold

you might not want to be a part of. Needless to say, I choose not to invest in this particular stock.

Placing an Order in a Fast-Trading Upward Market

If you try to buy an option at the ask price on the announcement, you will probably *not* get your order filled. The option prices change so rapidly on the news release that getting an order filled at the ask price is almost impossible. So, what should you do? You could place a *market order,* which means that you are willing to buy the call option at whatever price the market maker sets. However, this isn't always the best idea, because you will usually get a *bad fill* and end up overpaying for the option. Some investors choose to place market orders on great stock-split companies. I choose to set a limit order just above the last ask price, knowing that in a fast market I will get my order filled at that price instead of at a hyped-up, unrealistic price. You can't outsmart the market makers; they are in control; but you *can* set your limits. Normally, I will place a limit order of ⅛ or ¼ point above the ask price. If I get filled, I'm happy; if I don't, then I'll reconsider my options. If need be, I'll cancel my order and raise my price if the rally hasn't already begun.

If I have placed an order on the announcement and the order has not been filled within a few minutes, and the price is running up, I will have my broker place a *fill-or-kill* order. This tells the market maker to fill the order I placed as specified, or cancel it immediately. I don't want to leave the order sitting there as the market passes up my buy price, because the option prices may drop, and my order would then get filled on the downward movement, as the news fades away.

Common Sense is perhaps the most equally divided, but surely the most underemployed talent in the world.

—Christiane Collange

Figure 7.3   Confirmation slips of Sterling Software options trade

You Bought
Trade Date 03/11/98 for Settlement on 03/12/98

Quantity 10	Price 2 1/4	Settlement Amount
Description: CALL STERLING SOFTWARE IN AT 55 EXPIRES 04-18-1998 OPENING UNSOLICITED TRADE		Principal $2,250.00 Commission 68.25 H/P/I 2.35 Trans Fee 7.00 Net Amount $2,327.60 **BOUGHT** Security No. 4T222 Symbol CSSWAP55

You Sold
Trade Date 03/12/98 for Settlement on 03/13/98

Quantity 10	Price 3 3/8	Settlement Amount
Description: CALL STERLING SOFTWARE IN AT 55 EXPIRES 04-18-1998 CLOSING UNSOLICITED TRADE		Principal $3,375.00 Commission 112.72 S.E.C. Fee 0.12 H/P/I 2.35 Trans Fee 7.00 Net Amount $3,252.81 **SOLD** **PROFIT $ 925.21** Security No. 4T222 Symbol CSSWAP55

The right man is the one who seizes the moment.

—Johann Wolfgang von Goethe

Figure 7.4   Confirmation slips of BMC Software options trade

You Bought
Trade Date 04/21/98 for Settlement on 04/22/98

Quantity	10	Price	3.00	Settlement Amount

Description:
CALL BMC SOFTWARE   AT 100 EXPIRES 05-16-1998
OPENING

   UNSOLICITED TRADE

Principal $3,000.00
Commission   72.85
H/P/I   2.35
Trans Fee   7.00

Net Amount $3,082.20

BOUGHT

Security No. 5Y742
Symbol CBCQMY00

You Sold
Trade Date 04/21/98 for Settlement on 04/22/98

Quantity	10	Price	4 1/2	Settlement Amount

Description:
CALL BMC SOFTWARE   AT 100 EXPIRES 05-16-1998
CLOSING

Principal $4,500.00
Commission   123.05
S.E.C. Fee   0.15
H/P/I   2.35
Trans Fee   7.00

Net Amount $4,367.45

SOLD

PROFIT $ 1,285.25

Security No. 5Y742
Symbol CBCQMY00

Profit = $ 1,285.25

Possess your soul with patience.

—John Dryden

Figure 7.5　Confirmation slips of Mastech options trade

You Bought
Trade Date 03/17/98 for Settlement on 03/18/98

Quantity 10	Price 2 3/4	Settlement Amount
Description: CALL MASTECH CORP OPENING UNSOLICITED TRADE	AT 60 EXPIRES 04-18-1998	Principal　　　　$2,750.00 Commission　　　　71.32 H/P/I　　　　　　2.35 Trans Fee　　　　7.00 Net Amount　　$2,830.67 **BOUGHT** Security No. 0BK40 Symbol CQACAP60

You Sold
Trade Date 03/17/98 for Settlement on 03/18/98

Quantity 10	Price 3 1/2	Settlement Amount
Description: CALL MASTECH CORP CLOSING UNSOLICITED TRADE	AT 60 EXPIRES 04-18-1998	Principal　　　　$3,500.00 Commission　　　　75.91 S.E.C. Fee　　　　0.12 H/P/I　　　　　　2.35 Trans Fee　　　　7.00 Net Amount　　$3,414.62 **SOLD** **PROFIT $　583.95** Security No. 0BK40 Symbol CQACAP60

Life is the faculty of spontaneous activity, the awareness that we have powers.

—Immanuel Kant

By placing the fill-or-kill order, I set several things in motion:

- I should get a response within a couple of minutes from the market maker, verifying that my order was filled.

- If my order was filled, I can quickly place an order to sell my option for approximately $0.50 to $1.00 more than what I paid for it. This allows me to sell the option within the 15 minutes and catch the hype of the inflated options.

- If my order was not filled, I can decide if I want to pay more for the option or stand on the sidelines and wait for the dipping undervalued calls (DUC) play, as described in the next chapter.

- If for some reason I received a bad fill as the options quickly deflated, I can now give my broker a path of recourse to see if the transaction can be canceled.

In a fast-trading market, don't assume your trade has been made unless your broker can confirm it. So, if you try to cancel your order, don't be surprised if you can't. The key is to know what to do and how to react. Figures 7.1 to 7.5 show charts and confirmation slips of successful trades using this strategy for Theragenics, BMC Software, Sterling Software, and Mastech.

The plan for this strategy is to be in and out of the trade within 15 minutes, *maximum*. After the first 15 minutes, the hype begins to die down, and the call option prices begin to deflate quickly. Don't assume that all stock-split announcements are money makers. Knowing how to react is the key to placing a profitable trade on the announcement of a stock split during market hours. This strategy can also be played with news-related information, such as FDA approvals, mergers, acquisitions, and other breaking news.

Necessity of action takes away the fear of the act, and makes bold resolution the favorite of fortune.

—Francis Quarles

chapter 8

strategy 3: postannouncement dipping undervalued calls (duc)

The dipping undervalued calls (DUC) play normally takes place about three days after Strategy 2 (the stock-split announcement). Approximately three days (or sooner) after the stock-split announcement, the stock will pull back and drop in value. This usually happens for two reasons. The first reason is profit taking by wise investors, large investment firms, and corporate fund managers. The second reason is that the stock has tested its higher resistance level and lost its hype as the news was released.

Usually, nine out of ten stocks show signs of a sell-off immediately after the stock split has been announced. Being able to

---

Choose stocks the way the porcupines make love
—very carefully.

—Anonymous

determine the exact point of entry will determine how soon and how much of a profit can be made. Wait for the falling piano to hit the bottom and begin to bounce before purchasing the stock or option. If you wouldn't catch a falling piano, then don't buy the stock or option as it is falling. Allow the stock to hit its support level. It is at this point that it is an ideal entry point to buy in. Using charts makes it easier for you to identify the sell-off. Stocks that pull back in value normally show a pattern of trading sideways. *Trading sideways* simply means that there is consistently a very small upward and downward movement in the stock before breaking out to the upside. Indications of how much the stock will pull back or trade sideways can be determined several ways. Two of the biggest factors are the stock-split ratio and the actual stock-split date.

The *stock-split ratio* helps the volatility of the stock if the ratio is more favorable—for example, 2-for-1 and 3-for-1 splits. Other split ratios, such as 3-for-2 or 4-for-2, usually do not create as much interest, which, in turn, means less volatility.

The *stock-split date,* known as the ex-dividend date (ex-date)—the last chance to purchase the stock and receive the split dividend—appears to be the most important determining factor, due to the fact that it will usually determine the length of a DUC play. It is very common for a company to release the actual split date at the same time as the split announcement.

In the past, the split date would usually take place anywhere from 30 to 180 days after the date of the split announcement. In today's market, it is unusual for a company to wait any longer than 60 days after the split announcement. The most common time frame between split announcement and split date is 30 days or less. It is my opinion that corporate

---

All progress has resulted from people
who take unpopular positions.

—Adlai Stevenson

Figure 8.1   Microsoft Corporation (MSFT) chart showing DUC play. (*TC 2000* chart courtesy of Worden Brothers, Inc.)

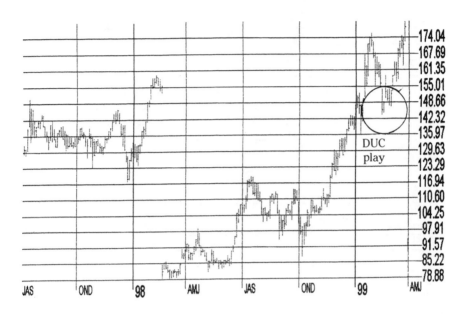

directors have realized that a strong momentum in the stock is created by decreasing the number of days between the split announcement and the split date. When viewing charts, note that momentum comes from the short time frames between the split announcement and the ex-date. Stocks with less momentum usually tend to have more than one DUC play.

Now, having said that, let's get back to determining when to "pull the trigger" (buy in) and go for the DUC. As I've said repeatedly, you need to rely on the charts to give you the buy signal. To be reassured, I personally like to wait until the stock

It's a funny thing about life: If you refuse to accept anything but the very best, you will very often get it.

—W. Somerset Maugham

Figure 8.2 Wal-Mart (WMT) chart showing DUC play. (*TC 2000 chart courtesy of Worden Brothers, Inc.*)

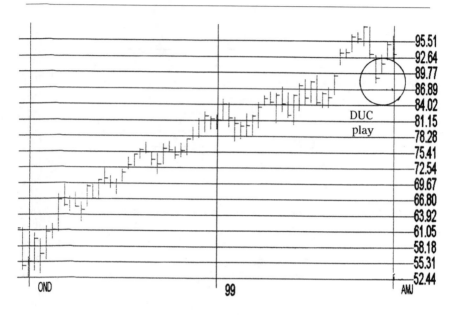

has closed in positive territory three consecutive days in a row. This is a very bullish sign and usually indicates that the stock will continue moving in an upward trend.

Now that you have indications of a strong upward movement, your next decision is whether to purchase the stock or the call option. When you are buying call options, it is best to purchase in-the-money options with a *delta* of 70 percent or more. The delta is the percentage your options increase for each dollar the stock increases. If the stock is trading in a nice upward trend and your option has plenty of time, you may want to hold your position through Strategy 4, the presplit run, dis-

*All men command patience, although few be willing
to practice it.*

—Thomas à Kempis

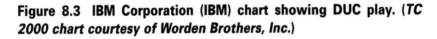

Figure 8.3   IBM Corporation (IBM) chart showing DUC play. (*TC 2000 chart courtesy of Worden Brothers, Inc.*)

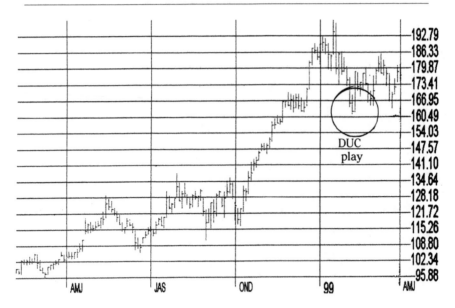

cussed in the next chapter. When purchasing the options, allow for approximately three months of time and set a safe exit point close to the last resistance level. More important, make sure your call option expiration date is at least one month beyond the split date to be safe. If you decide to purchase the stock, your only other decision is then when to sell. Successful DUCs (stocks) leave their resting pond (support level) and fly upward. When a DUC spends too much time in the pond, it is best to move on to another investment.

The charts for Microsoft (Figure 8.1), Wal-Mart (Figure 8.2), and IBM (Figure 8.3) show perfect examples of DUC plays.

It's a wonderful feeling when you discover some evidence to support your beliefs.

—Anonymous

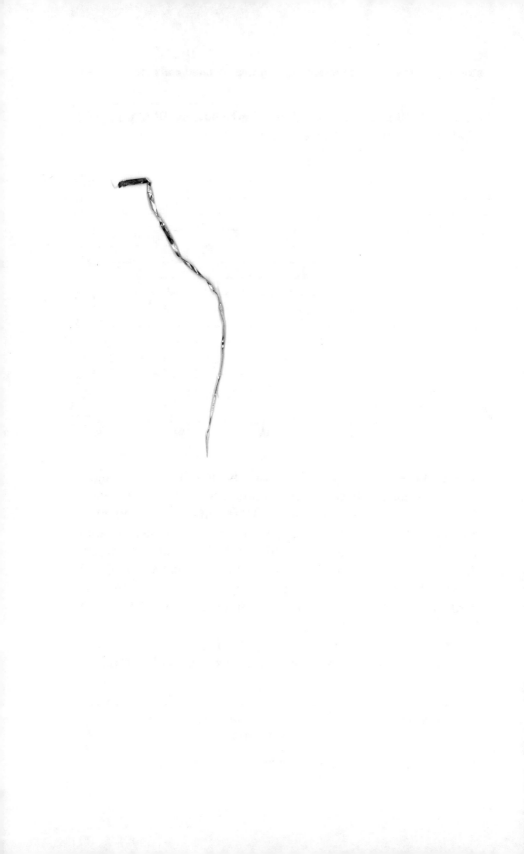

chapter 9

strategy 4: presplit

The presplit run, otherwise known as the pay date, is a short-term play, made one to three days before the date of the stock split. I believe the reason that stocks tend to have this run-up is because there are investors who feel that this is the best time to take advantage of the stock, before its actual split price. Yet if you were to wait until after the split, you could buy the stock at half the price. Technically, the stock price would be the same, but if you have a limited amount of money to invest it is more affordable after the split. Regardless of the reason, it works for me.

To prove this strategy, look at stock splits through your charting service. Viewing the charts enables you to see the

---

I'm overpaying myself, and I'm worth it.

—Mark Larson

Figure 9.1 Doubleclick (DCLK) chart showing presplit run. *(TC 2000 chart courtesy of Worden Brothers, Inc.)*

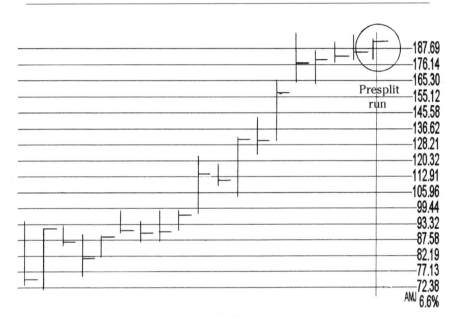

results of the run-up on the previous pay dates. If the stock is trading sideways or downward on the third day before the pay date, it is not wise to place the trade. If the stock doesn't break out to the upside that day, you should check the stock movement at the next market opening and then make the trade, provided that the stock is moving upward. Each and every trade you make should be for a purpose. Strategy 4 should be played only when you can identify the upward movement.

An ideal entry time for this play is when that individual stock is trading upward even though the overall market is not.

Take calculated risks. That is quite different from being rash.

—George S. Patton

Figure 9.2 Lucent Technologies (LU) chart showing presplit run. *(TC 2000 chart courtesy of Worden Brothers, Inc.)*

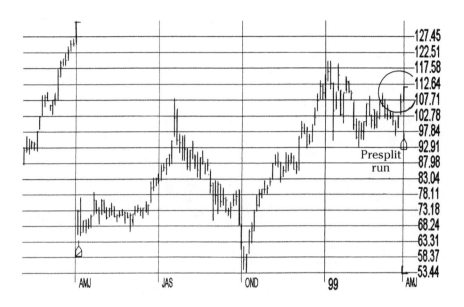

As I like to say, it's not always the overall market conditions that affect my trades, it's the *purpose* of my trades. If the market is moving upward on the same day as Strategy 4, you may see a more rewarding profit sooner than expected. Being that this is a short-term trade, look to make about ½ to 1 point on the day that the position is opened. When trading the option, it is wise to buy 10 contracts, find the small movement, and get out.

You may choose to buy the stock; personally, I usually purchase the in-the-money call option. I buy as far in the money as possible to be assured that I'm getting as much *delta*

The trouble with being poor is that it takes up all your time.

—Willem De Kooning

Figure 9.3 Microsoft Corporation (MSFT) chart showing presplit run. *(TC 2000 chart courtesy of Worden Brothers, Inc.)*

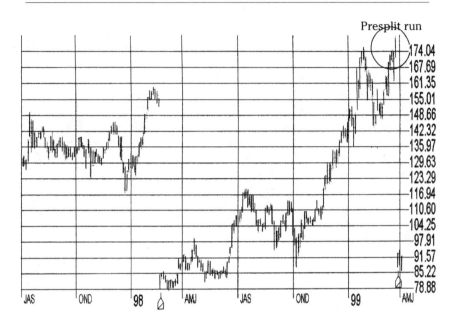

(percentage ratio the option moves for each dollar the stock moves) on my option as possible. I like to see that I'm receiving a minimum delta of 75 percent. If you're trading the stock, it will be a dollar-for-dollar movement.

When buying the stock, you don't have to decide what month option to purchase, as you do when you trade the option. When buying the option, it is safer to pay for the extra time, as you'll see it works to your advantage. If the current-month option has at least two weeks of time left, I'll usually buy that option knowing exactly when I'm going to sell.

The best time to take your profit is the trading day before

This is America. You can do anything here.

—Robert Edward Turner III

the stock splits, just before the market closes. Many times the stock will have a quick run-up just toward the closing of the day. However, if the company is a larger well-known company such as America Online (AOL), Microsoft (MSFT), Wal-Mart (WMT), or Cisco Systems (CSCO), it may be wise to hold on to your position until after the split—especially if the split day is the very next trading day and not the Monday after the weekend. Well-known companies have a tendency to continue upward after the actual split.

When holding your positions until after the split, be sure to use trailing stop losses. If you choose to hold your options until after the split, your options are treated just like the stock; they will split in the same ratio as the stock.

Example

2-for-1 Stock Split

	Before Split	*After Split*
Stock	100 shares at $100 per share	200 shares at $50 per share
Option	10 contracts at $700 per contract	20 contracts at $350 per contract

If the stock splits at a ratio of 2 for 1, you will have 200 shares (double). When the stock splits, the price value also splits, giving you a price value of $50 per share (half of the presplit stock price value). The same applies to the option; a 2-for-1 split will give you 20 contracts (double), giving you a price value of $350 per contract (half of the presplit option value). This means that your cost base of both the stock and option split in half. If you paid $100 per share for the stock, your cost base is now $50 per share, and if you paid $700 per

---

It is easier to get out than to stay out.

—Mark Twain

Figure 9.4   Confirmation slips of Microsoft options trade based on chart shown in Figure 9.3

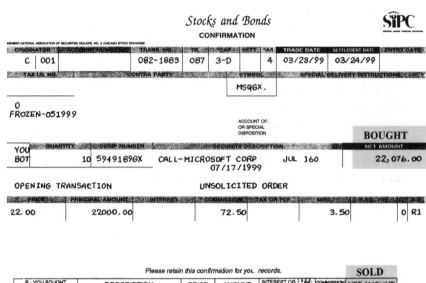

contract for the option, your cost base per contract is now $350. I don't mind holding on to the well-known companies after the split due to the fact that many investors will look at these stocks as being half price and very affordable—which, in turn, drives the stock price up.

There is nothing wrong with chance, if it is in the right direction.

—Winston Churchill

If you choose to hold on to your investment after the split, be careful—the upward trend may continue for only about 1 to 3 days. Somewhere during this time frame, many postsplit stocks have a tendency to pull back down by about 5 percent of the stock's value. After a stock has pulled back, and it establishes a new support level, you need to get ready to position yourself for Strategy 5, postsplit dipping undervalued call (DUC), discussed in the next chapter.

Figures 9.1 to 9.4 show charts and confirmation slips of successful trades using this strategy for Doubleclick, Lucent, and Microsoft.

The key to Strategy 4 is the same as that to the others— the *purpose,* which is to get in and out as soon as possible and take a small profit, ranging from $500 to $1,000. Remember to have your predetermined stop-loss order, so that if the stock goes against you, you're out. If you decide to hold your position through the split, and the stock price gaps up on the opening day of the new stock price (split price), it is wise to take your profits and get out.

The purpose is the eternal condition of success.

—Theodore T. Munger

chapter 10

strategy 5: postsplit dipping undervalued calls (duc)

The postsplit dipping undervalued calls (DUC) play is also known as the range rider. I use the term *range rider* throughout this chapter, defining it as a stock that has the potential to return to its previous (52-week high) price within 12 to 16 months after the actual split. The term *range rider* comes from the image of a person on horseback who rides up to the highest peaks of the mountains. Both the rider and the stock take off from level ground, with the intention of reaching the peak as soon as possible.

More investors would invest in range riders if they knew that, based on a study at Harvard University, about 90 percent

---

Dreams never hurt anybody if he keeps working right behind the dreams to make as much of them become real as he can.

—Frank W. Woolworth

of stock-split companies return back to their previous split price within 16 months. It didn't take a university study to convince me; I just looked at the pictures (that is, the charts). I have stated earlier in this book that a picture is worth thousands of dollars—well, this is the picture that proves it.

Once again, one way to invest is to buy the stock and hold it throughout the run-up. However, back to having specialized knowledge, I would much rather invest in the option, rather than the stock. Refreshing your memory, remember that options are not available for each month because they are sold on a yearly cycle. If you want to invest, you should buy a call option that has a minimum of six months time. Meaning, you should select an expiration date that is at least six months after the split date. If you find that a certain month is not available because of the cycle, choose the next available month.

Strike prices have now split as the stock did. So, are there certain strike prices you should or shouldn't purchase? Truthfully, I don't think it makes much of a difference other than that the deeper in the money you are, the more intrinsic value you have. I prefer to tie up less money by trading the out-of-the-money options, this being a long-term investment. Spend less money when buying the out-of-the-money option and buy yourself more time, as you are anticipating that the stock will run back to its previous split price.

Speaking of time, after the stock has split I like to make a long-term investment, yet I don't buy the stock. I need to rephrase that: I make a long-term investment, but I do *not* own the stock. I use what are called *LEAPS options.*

Long-term equity anticipation securities (LEAPS) are long-

Remember that your wealth can be measured,
not by what you have, but by what you are.

—Unknown

term equity options traded on U.S. exchanges and over the counter. Instead of expiring in near-term months as most equities do, LEAPS expire in two or three years, giving the buyer's strategy a longer time to become more profitable.

LEAPS are no different from any other stock option, other than that they are available only two years out at a time, and that all LEAPS options expire on the third Friday of January of each year. LEAPS are no longer considered LEAPS options when there is less than six months remaining before their expiration. As an example, let's say it's now March 2000—the only options available are for January 2001 and January 2002. The LEAPS options for the year 2003 will become available 6 months before the January 2001 expiration.

So, if a stock has the potential to return back to its previous split price within 12 to 16 months, then why not buy the LEAPS options? You're probably thinking that it would cost a lot more money to do so, but the reality is that it doesn't. If you do the math (divide the number of months by the cost of the option), you'll find that more often than not, it is not only wiser, but also cheaper. Volatility plays a large part, as well as liquidity. Few investors spend money on options because of the *risk,* yet they'll buy the stock and hold on to it for several years. As my knowledge in the stock market continues to expand, I still have to say that LEAPS are my favorite strategy overall, for the following reasons:

- The cost of the LEAPS option is much less than that of owning the stock.
- LEAPS enable you to diversify in different sectors, with less expense.

The only place success comes before work is in the dictionary.

—Vidal Sassoon

- The value of the LEAPS may not drop as much as the stock value.
- LEAPS have the same rewards when the stock splits.
- LEAPS allow for a monthly income (calendar spreads).
- There is less financial risk if the value of the stock drastically drops.
- LEAPS still give you the right to buy the stock at your predetermined option strike price prior to expiration.

If LEAPS don't excite you, you might need to check your vitamin level. When I first learned about LEAPS I thought they were too good to be true until I bought and sold my America Online (AOL) LEAPS for a monthly profit of $22,585.65, as shown in Figure 10.1. Now, that is a *great* rate of return on my investment for the cost.

I say *for the cost* because, if I hadn't had the knowledge, I wouldn't have had the money available to purchase 1,000 shares of the stock. At the time, it was trading around $80 per share (1,000 × $80 = $80,000). My cost for the January 2000, $85 strike price was $25,250 (10 contracts = 1,000 shares × $25.25 per share = $25,250). This qualifies for the option being less expensive than owning the stock, and yet I still controlled 1,000 shares, as did the stock investor.

This strategy enables me to diversify, so I am able to own more LEAPS in a different sector. Why other sectors? Different types of businesses have a tendency to move in different directions at different times. So, if the tech sector isn't moving, maybe the retail sector is. When you own the stock and the stock value drops, your investment value drops dollar for dollar. But depending on the strike price and expiration of the

---

Money is something you got to make in case you don't die.

—Max Asnas

Figure 10.1   Confirmation slips of America Online, Inc. (AOL) LEAPS options trade based on chart shown in Figure 10.3a.

Stocks and Bonds

CONFIRMATION

SIPC

MEMBER NATIONAL ASSOCIATION OF SECURITIES DEALERS, INC. & CHICAGO STOCK EXCHANGE

ORIGINATOR	ACCOUNT NUMBER	TRANS. NO.	TR.	*CAP.	SETT.	*A/I	TRADE DATE	SETTLEMENT DATE	ENTRY DATE
C 001		323-0514	087	3-D		4	11/19/98	11/20/98	

TAX I.D. NO.	CONTRA PARTY	SYMBOL	SPECIAL DELIVERY INSTRUCTIONS
		LOLAQ.	

ACCOUNT OF:
OR SPECIAL
DISPOSITION.

	QUANTITY	CUSIP NUMBER	SECURITY DESCRIPTION	NET AMOUNT
YOU BOT	10	02364JOAQ	CALL-AMERICA ONLINE INC JAN 85 01/22/2000	25,346.75

BOUGHT

OPENING TRANSACTION   UNSOLICITED ORDER

PRICE	PRINCIPAL AMOUNT	INTEREST	COMMISSION	TAX OR FCP	MISC.	S.E.C. FEE	A-E
25 1/4	25250.00		93.25			3.50	D R1

Stocks and Bonds

CONFIRMATION

SIPC

MEMBER NATIONAL ASSOCIATION OF SECURITIES DEALERS, INC. & CHICAGO STOCK EXCHANGE

ORIGINATOR	ACCOUNT NUMBER	TRANS. NO.	TR.	*CAP.	SETT.	*A/I	TRADE DATE	SETTLEMENT DATE	ENTRY DATE
C 001		355-1025	087	3-D		J	12/21/98	12/22/98	

TAX I.D. NO.	CONTRA PARTY	SYMBOL	SPECIAL DELIVERY INSTRUCTIONS

ACCOUNT OF:
OR SPECIAL
DISPOSITION

PROFIT $22,585.65

	QUANTITY	CUSIP NUMBER	SECURITY DESCRIPTION	NET AMOUNT
YOU SLD	10	02364JOAQ	CALL-AMERICA ONLINE INC JAN 85 01/22/2000	47,932.40

SOLD

CLOSING TRANSACTION   UNSOLICITED ORDER

PRICE	PRINCIPAL AMOUNT	INTEREST	COMMISSION	TAX OR FCP	MISC.	S.E.C. FEE	A-E
48.00	48000.00		62.50		9.50	1.60	R R1

The true measure of your worth includes all the benefits others have gained from your success.

—Cullen Hightower

option, your LEAPS may not drop as much in value, because most of your premium is based on the stock's anticipated performance before the long-term expiration of the LEAPS.

The LEAPS option will perform the same as the stock does when it splits. As covered earlier, your option strike price, the number of contracts, and your cost base will split in the same ratio as the stock. So, if you're holding long-term LEAPS, you benefit each time the stock splits. Carefully view the Microsoft (MSFT) LEAPS illustrated in Figure 10.2.

Example

You bought 2-year LEAPS for 1,000 shares of Microsoft (equal to 10 contracts) for a $200 strike price:

$$1,000 \text{ shares} \times \$200 \text{ per share} = \$20,000$$

If Microsoft continues to split (2 for 1) on an average of every 12 months, and you bought the long-term LEAPS just before the split date, your 10 contracts become 20, then 40, then 80, as outlined in Figure 10.2a. Your strike price changes from $200 to $100 and then $50. Your original investment of $20,000 increases to $100,000, then $260,000, and so on.

Figure 10.1 shows a copy of the AOL LEAPS I bought just after it split (as shown in Figure 10.3a); when it ran up, I could not help but hear the little man in the back of my mind saying *sell, sell, sell*—so I did. Figures 10.3b to 10.5 also show charts of postsplit runs for Home Depot, Lucent, Pfizer, Cisco, and Dell.

Although my purpose in buying the AOL LEAPS was to sell calls (known as calendar spreads) against the LEAPS option, I couldn't allow myself not to take the profit. I'm not going to cover selling calls against LEAPS; many books are available on

---

You only live once, but if you work it right, once is enough.

—Joe E. Lewis

Figure 10.2 Postsplit play in Microsoft Corporation (MSFT) LEAPS: (a) summary of LEAPS at splits and run-ups, (b) graph of points covered in summary, and (c) chart of MSFT showing splits and postsplit run. (TC 2000 chart courtesy of Worden Brothers, Inc.)

Graph Point	MSFT	Strike Price	Total Contracts	Cost	Value	Market Value
1	$160	$200	10	$20	$20	$20,000

Stock splits 2 for 1 down to $80 on February 23 (ex-dividend date):

Graph Point	MSFT	Strike Price	Total Contracts	Cost	Value	Market Value
2	$80	$100	20	$10	$10	$20,000

Assume the stock rises $80 back to $160—the LEAPS, with a delta of 50 percent, will increase by $40 to $50:

Graph Point	MSFT	Strike Price	Total Contracts	Cost	Value	Market Value
3	$160	$100	20	$10	$50	$100,000

The stock again splits 2 for 1 down to $80:

Graph Point	MSFT	Strike Price	Total Contracts	Cost	Value	Market Value
4	$80	$50	40	$5	$25	$100,000

Assume the stock again rises from $80 to $160:

Graph Point	MSFT	Strike Price	Total Contracts	Cost	Value	Market Value
5	$160	$50	40	$5	$65	$260,000

Then, if it splits for a third time:

Graph Point	MSFT	Strike Price	Total Contracts	Cost	Value	Market Value
6	$80	$25	80	$2.50	$32.50	$260,000

(a)

Figure 10.2 (Continued)

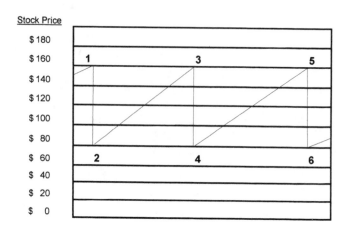

(b)

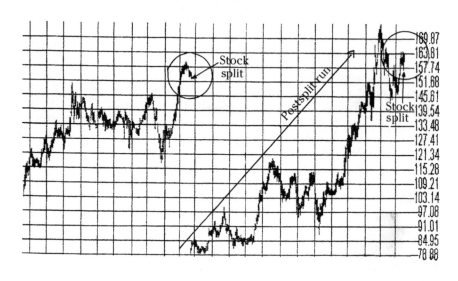

(c)

Figure 10.3 Charts showing stock-split patterns and postsplit runs: (*a*) America Online, Inc. (AOL), and (*b*) Home Depot, Inc. (HD). (*TC 2000 charts courtesy of Worden Brothers, Inc.)

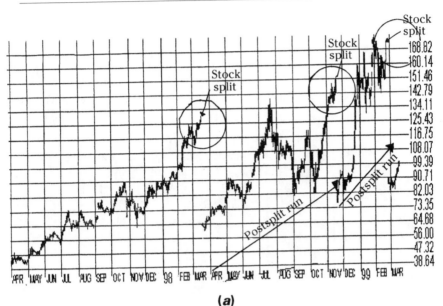

(*a*)

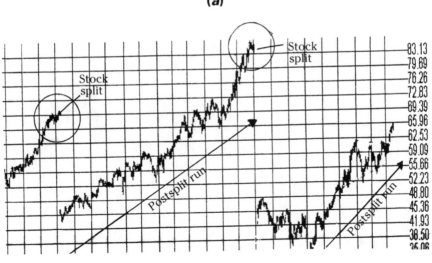

(*b*)

**Figure 10.4 Charts showing stock-split patterns and postsplit runs: (*a*) Lucent Technologies (LU), and (*b*) Pfizer, Inc. (PFE). *(TC 2000 charts courtesy of Worden Brothers, Inc.)*

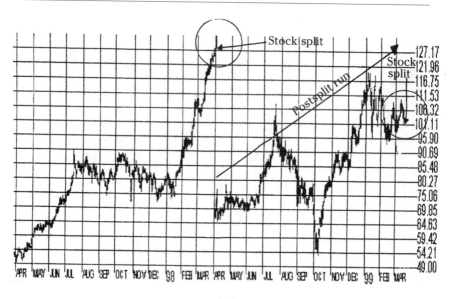

(*a*)

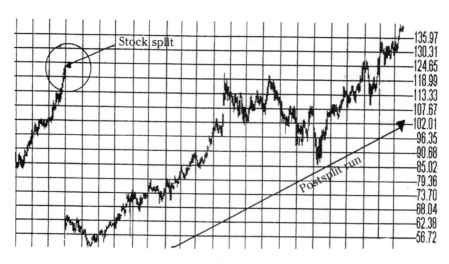

(*b*)

Figure 10.5 Charts showing stock-split patterns and postsplit runs: (*a*) Cisco Systems (CSCO), and (*b*) Dell Computer Corporation (DELL). *(TC 2000 charts courtesy of Worden Brothers, Inc.)*

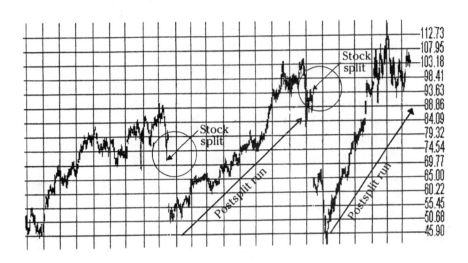

(a)

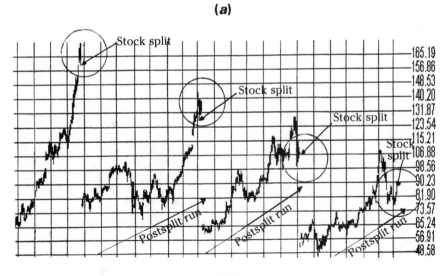

(b)

Figure 10.6 Five times to get involved in stock-split companies and how to play each: (1) Buy long-term call options—3 to 6 months, slightly in or out of the money. Buy 7 to 10 days before board of directors meeting—sell on news. (2) Buy short-term call options—1 to 5 weeks, in the money. Buy within seconds of announcement. Sell for small profit (or loss) within 1 or 2 hours. (3) Buy call, after dip on upward movement, for next expiration after split date, in the money. Set GTC for $1 or so profit; wait and do it again. (4) Buy short-term call options—2 to 5 *weeks,* in the money. Buy 3 to 7 business days before split on upward movement. Sell when goal is hit, but before split. (5) Buy long-term LEAPS options—on upward movement, slightly in or out of the money. Set GTC for realistic profit. Adjust upward if move continues. Set trailing stops.

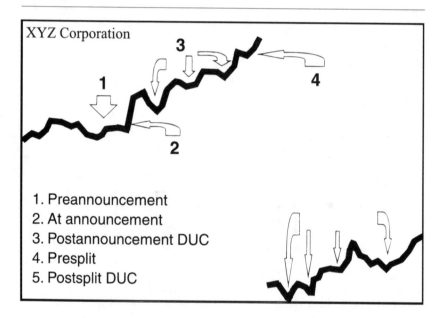

XYZ Corporation

1. Preannouncement
2. At announcement
3. Postannouncement DUC
4. Presplit
5. Postsplit DUC

An unaspiring person believes according to what he achieves.
An aspiring person achieves according to what he believes.

—Sri Chinmoy

such strategies as *writing covered calls* and *calendar spreads.* These advanced strategies allow you to sell calls against the stock or options you own, and in doing so you collect a monthly premium. When writing covered calls you do so to get called out—and if you're not called out, that's fine, as you will keep a premium and still own the stock. However, with calendar spreads you *can't* allow yourself to get called out, or you will *lose* the time premium you paid for your option.

Stock-split investments are bullish trades, and when they are going in your direction you may find it is possible to play each and every one of the five stock-split strategies covered so far, as outlined in Figure 10.6. Some stocks may have shorter or longer runs, so it is best to trade the ones that have the highest stock volume with a more attractive looking chart. If these stocks show a good, strong pattern and continue above a certain price, take advantage of the running bull. A great strategy for running bulls is the *bull put spread,* the subject of the next chapter.

The idea in this game isn't to win popularity polls or to be a good guy to everyone. The name of the game is win.

—Billy Martin

chapter 11

strategy 6:
bull put spreads

This strategy may be the toughest strategy to understand, so if you do not fully understand bull put spreads, you might want to slowly read through this chapter a second time. Personally, I had a very difficult time understanding not only what a bull put spread was, but how to place a bull put spread order with my broker. Not all brokers are familiar with this strategy, so if you haven't been able to find the most educated broker for option trading and bull put spreads, I suggest that you either give a copy of this book to your broker or stick to online trading.

Understanding bull put spreads is a challenging way of making a lot of money on a monthly basis. This strategy is very

---

The surest way not to fail is to determine to succeed.

—Richard Brinsley Sheridan

rewarding for me. It nets me, personally, an average of about $1,250 per month by implementing just one spread.

As I travel throughout the country talking to different investors about the stock market, I have found that even experienced traders do not fully understand bull put spreads. So, with that thought in mind, I will do my best to explain them in the simplest terms.

You may find that some of the information covered here is repetitious of other chapters, but I feel it is necessary to review it as it pertains to bull put spreads. My goal in this chapter is to give you enough knowledge and confidence to be able to implement bull put spreads immediately. But again, I suggest that you spend some time paper trading before using your hard-earned money in real trades.

I love to implement bull put spreads on companies doing stock splits because I have never been wrong. Yes, you read correctly, I have *never* been wrong. Every time I have placed a bull put spread trade with a stock-split announcement, I have profited. The key to the profits is in the research.

We all know that the stock market is very risky, and we can't always be right—but what if you were wrong and still made money? You're probably thinking, "This guy is crazy, he should see a doctor!" I thought the same thing before I realized the power of bull put spreads.

The first step is to do your homework. Check the charts and the indicators to see if the stock is on a positive upward trend. This is the opportune time to place a bull put spread. Keep in mind that spreads are strictly a short-term option strategy.

Earlier I mentioned that the key to success is not how much money you have, but how much *specialized knowledge*

He was a self-made man who owed his lack
of success to nobody.

—Joseph Heller

you have. Well, this chapter presents a perfect example of the power behind having specialized knowledge. Now, read on as I explain bull put spreads, and then decide if you think I should see a doctor.

Keep in mind, throughout this chapter, that I'm referring to placing bull put spreads on companies that are about to announce or have just announced a stock split. There are other reasons to place bull put spreads, but since you've already taken the time to research stock-split candidates and bought call options with the anticipation of the stock going up, then why not make more money for being right? And if you're not right, then why not protect your losses by knowing how to turn the bull put spread into a profitable trade?

The term *bull* refers to being bullish on the stock. *Bullish* means you like the stock and your research shows that the stock is going up (or, in some cases, is going to remain about the same).

To keep this chapter very simple, visualize a bull with his horns. Now visualize the bull fighting, thrusting his head up, and forcing his horns upon his opponent. Simple picture—now you can remember that when someone says they are bullish on a stock, they are looking for the stock to go *up*.

Now, visualize being *bearish*. Picture a bear protecting itself. A bear reaches out with its paws, and claws downwards, when attacked. Simply put, being bearish means you are looking for the stock to go *down*. This may be simple, but the thing that has made me successful in the stock market is keeping things simple and always remembering the basics. We tend to forget the basics with more knowledge, but the basics are what make the most sense (and dollars!). When in doubt, go back to the basics.

Success is never final.

—Winston Churchill

Now let's discuss the term *put*. When you *buy* a put, you do so with the anticipation that the stock will *drop*. The opposite applies when you *sell* a put—you are anticipating that the stock will *increase* in value. Buying and selling puts is the whole concept behind the bull put spread.

You sell a put when you are bullish on the stock with the anticipation that the stock will go up. In the ideal trade, upon expiration of the option, the stock would be trading above the strike price at which you sold the put. By selling the put, you sell someone the right to put the stock to you at that certain price, and, in return, they agree to pay you a premium. If the stock is trading below that price on the expiration date of the option, the stock can be put to you at that strike price. If the stock stays above your chosen strike price at expiration, you get to keep the premium and are no longer obligated to purchase the stock for the set price (strike price).

Example

You have *sold* 10 contracts (1,000 shares) of Allstate Insurance (ALL) June $95 puts for a 2¼ ($2.25) premium:

1,000 shares × $2.25 per share = $ 2,250 premium

In this example (see Figure 11.1), you have *sold* someone the right to put the stock to you for $95 on or before the expiration date of this option. The purpose for doing this is that you are willing to purchase the stock at that price. If the stock is trading above the $95 strike price, the stock will not be put to you. The idea behind *selling* a put is wanting the stock to go up. The idea behind *buying* a put is wanting the stock to go down.

If only God would give me some clear sign! Like making a deposit in my name in a Swiss bank account.

—Woody Allen

Figure 11.1 Confirmation slips of Allstate Insurance (ALL) bull put spread trades

Quantity 10	Price 2 1/4	Settlement Amount

Description:
PUT ALLSTATE CORP   AT 95 EXPIRES 06-20-1998
OPENING

    UNSOLICITED TRADE

Principal	$2,250.00
Commission	69.62
S.E.C. Fee	0.08
Trans Fee	7.00
Net Amount	$2,173.30
	SOLD

Security No. 0QC73
Symbol PALLJN95

You Bought
Trade Date 05/19/98 for Settlement on 05/20/98

Quantity 10	Price 13/16	Settlement Amount

Description:
PUT ALLSTATE CORP   AT 90 EXPIRES 06-20-1998
OPENING

    UNSOLICITED TRADE

Principal	$812.50
Commission	49.37
H/P/I	2.35
Trans Fee	5.50
Net Amount	$869.72
	BOUGHT
	PROFIT $ 1,303.58

Security No. 6H672
Symbol PALLJN90

Keep your eyes on the stars, and your feet on the ground.

—Theodore Roosevelt

If the stock is trading at $97 per share on the day of expiration, the seller won't exercise their option of putting the stock to you for $95 when they could sell the stock in the open market for $97. If they did, they would lose the difference of the two prices, which in this example would be $2 per share.

Now, let's say the stock is trading below $95. You sold the put, so now someone has the right to put the stock to you at the $95 strike price. If the stock is at $93, you need to make a decision on your put option by the close of the market on or before the expiration date. Here are your three choices:

- You can allow the 10 contracts (1,000 shares) of stock to be put to you for the price of $95 per share (1,000 shares × $95 per share = $95,000).
- You can buy back the put you sold (which will cost you money if the stock drops much below the strike price you sold).
- You can buy back the put and roll out to the next month by selling the put again.

Selling puts is also known as being in a *naked* position because you sell an investment that you don't actually own at the time of the sale. If you are going to sell puts, then remember these three important rules:

Rule 1: It is a *very* risky strategy.

Rule 2: Be sure you know *exactly* what you are doing.

Rule 3: When selling puts, you should want to own the stock at the strike price you sold the put for.

The million little things that drop into our hands,
the small opportunities each day brings. He leaves us free
to use or abuse and goes unchanging along His silent way.

—Helen Keller

When selling a put, it is not always because you want the stock to be put to you at a lower price; in this example, it is to collect the premium.

The first step in understanding a bull put spread is to understand selling puts. Many people who like certain stocks use this strategy to buy stock that they want to own—but if the stock is not put to them, they still keep the premium.

Say you sold the $95 put, and come the expiration date, the stock is trading at $94. You now have the right to buy the stock at $95. The stock value is only $94, but you collected the $2.25 per share premium when you originally sold the put. So, really, your cost to own the stock is $95 minus the $2.25 premium, or $92.75. This is your cost base on the stock. In other words, you have just bought the stock at a discount, and, if you choose, you can turn around and sell the stock for $94 (market price) or, better yet, write a covered call for the next month out (another option strategy).

Most brokerage firms require that you hold about 30 percent of the total stock price for margin. If the stock is in the high-tech sector, many brokers require 50 percent or more, due to the risks involved with high-tech and Internet industries. Then again, there are many brokers who will not allow you to sell puts at all because they are risky. What I can't understand is, if you like the stock, and you wouldn't mind owning the stock at $95, then why wouldn't they let you buy it at a discount? Maybe it is just plain lack of knowledge on their behalf.

If you *bought the stock* at $95 and it goes down a dollar, you will lose $1,000. But, if you sold the put, you have just saved yourself from losing $1,000, and you actually end up being profitable by $1.25 per share, or $1,250 for 10 contracts. You

---

We have only to move confidently in the direction of our dreams and live the life we have imagined to meet with a success unexpected in common hours.

—Henry Thoreau

received $2.25 per share ($2,250) when you sold the put, the stock drops to $94, and someone puts 1,000 shares to you at the $95 strike price.

Example

Stock's strike price when put to you	$95 \times 1,000 = $95,000$
Stock's trading price when put to you	$94 \times 1,000 = $94,000$
Real loss if you bought the stock at $95	$-\$1 \times 1,000 = -\$1,000$
Premium received when you sold the put	$2.25 \times 1,000 = $2,250$
Stock put to you at $95 when value is $94	$1.00 \times 1,000 = $1,000$
Profit	$1,250

As an investor, you should decide how risky selling put options is. The risk in selling the puts is that the stock could really drop in value and someone will then put the stock to you for less then the premium you took in, but this is no different from the risk you would take if you owned the stock.

Table 11.1 shows a list of several stocks at their current trading prices and the option premiums you would receive if you were to sell the puts on these companies. The purpose of selling puts is for the following reasons:

- Wanting the stock to stay above the strike price so the stock doesn't get put to you in order to keep the put premium

- Liking the stock at that strike price with the anticipation of buying the stock if it gets put to you

Dell, Wal-Mart, Microsoft, and America Online are good quality companies that many investors add to their portfolios. Table 11.1 lists their current stock prices, strike prices, and put

---

The love of learning and the love of money rarely meet.

—George Herbert

Table 11.1 March Put Premiums

Company	Stock Price	Strike Price	Put Premium
Dell Computer (DELL)	$ 42.75	$ 42.50	$1.00
Wal-Mart (WMT)	96.50	95.00	1.25
Microsoft (MSFT)	160.50	160.00	2.75
America Online (AOL)	95.75	95.00	1.00

premiums. These are the premiums that you would have collected if you sold the March put. Now look at the next example and study the difference between the stock being put to you and not being put to you. Note what would happen if the stock was not put to you. In each example you are selling 10 contracts, equaling 1,000 shares. The examples show current prices for the month of March, with only one week left before the March expiration. The next example of options will show the net cost base of each stock if 1,000 shares were put to you come the March expiration (third Friday of each month).

Example

You have sold 10 contracts (1,000 shares) of Dell Computer (DELL) March $42.50 puts, and collected $1.00 per share premium (1,000 × $1 = $1,000), giving you a cost base of $42.50 − $1.00 = $41.50 per share.

For every dollar the stock goes below $41.50, you would suffer a loss. However, you were willing to buy the stock at the price of $42.50 per share. So, you have actually saved $1,000,

If you want to know what God thinks about money, look at the people He gives it to.

—Yiddish proverb

which was the premium you took in when you originally sold the put. The nice thing is, if the stock closes above $42.50 after the March expiration date, you get to keep the $1,000. Oh, gee, you wanted to buy the stock? That's okay—you can console yourself with $1,000 profit for a 1-week trade.

If the stock were trading at $41.50, you would have gotten the stock put to you at $42.50 even though it was only worth $41.50. Technically, this would be a loss of $1 per share, if you bought the stock instead of selling the put first. By selling the put, you actually didn't lose money, because you received the $1 per share put premium.

If you are willing to buy a particular stock, it may make more sense to sell the put first and have it put to you, rather than buying the stock at its current price. Take IBM, for example. On expiration of March options, a major firm downgraded the stock. The stock dropped 9 points in 1 day. If you sold the put, you would have had the stock put to you, yet you would have had less of a loss because you received the put premium when you sold the put. This off sets your loss if you had just bought the stock at its current ask price.

In the following examples, you will notice that Wal-Mart, Microsoft, and America Online all closed above the selected strike prices. In this case you would have kept the full premium, since the stock was not put to you. It is important for you to remember that you should sell puts only on stocks that you wouldn't mind owning and at that strike price.

Dell, Wal-Mart, Microsoft, and America Online were trades made within one week prior to the expiration of the put options. To summarize: When selling puts on each of the companies, you receive the put premium in your account the next trading day. If you add up the put premiums, you would have received

---

Wise men learn by other men's mistakes, fools by their own.

—Anonymous

$6,000 (for 10 contracts) combined. After the expiration date, Dell was the only stock that was trading below its strike price. Wal-Mart, Microsoft, and America Online were all above the strike price. Come Monday, following the expiration, you would have been put 1,000 shares of Dell stock at $42.50 (your cost base is $41.50), and the remaining put options would have expired worthless, leaving you the total cash amount of $5,000. It should now be easier for you to understand why I like to sell puts on stocks that I wouldn't mind owning. And if I don't get the stock put to me, that's great too. To summarize, I made 4 trades with 1 week of time remaining, received 1,000 shares of Dell at a discount price, and collected $5,000 from stocks I didn't get to buy. I consider that a nice paycheck for the week.

Now, on the other side of the coin, what happens when stock really drops in value? Bull put spreads are considered to be safer in cases where the stock drops drastically, and I'll explain why. But, before I explain the second half of the bull put spread, I must first explain how to buy back or roll out of selling puts. This strategy is used when you do not want the stock to be put to you.

To recap: When you sell puts, you want the stock value to be above the strike price at expiration on the third Friday of that month—technically, at 12 P.M. on the Saturday following that Friday. You should sell puts only for that current month. Do not sell puts, or be placing bull put spreads, on future months! A lot can happen with more time.

By *rolling out,* you can defer your losses to the next month or turn the losses into a gain. Here's how. Say you sold the June $95 put, the expiration date is today, and the stock is trading at $94. The market is not moving in your favor, and it doesn't look

---

*There are more things in life to worry about than just money—
how to get ahold of it, for example.*

—Anonymous

like the stock will rise above $95 before the close. Even though you should sell puts only on stock you'd like to own, you decide you have changed your mind and no longer want to purchase the stock. When trading options, you can buy an option back after you have already sold it to close out your position. But make sure you buy the same strike price and month. I know this can get confusing. So, here's yet another example:

Example

Part 1: Sell put.

Shares (10 contracts)	1,000
Premium	× $2.25
In your account	$2,250

Part 2: Buy put (on expiration date).

Shares (10 contracts)	1,000
Premium	× $1.25
Out of your pocket	$1,250
Profit from selling put	$2,250
Cost to buy it back	–$1,250
Profit from changing your mind	$1,000

You sold 10 contracts (1,000 shares) of the June $95 put for $2.25 and received $2,225. Come expiration day, the stock is at $94, and you don't want the stock to be put to you. So, if you sold the June $95 put, you could buy it back and close out the position so the stock wouldn't be put to you.

In order to buy the put back, you will have to come up with the money because you are *buying* something. So, if the June $95 put cost $1.25 to buy back, you will have given back $1.25 of the $2.25 you received when you sold the put. You will

---

There are only two emotions of Wall Street—fear and greed.

—William M. LeFevre, Jr.

still end up with $1 per share profit, but more important, you have closed out the position so the stock won't be put to you. Simply put: If you sold a put you would buy back the put to close out the position, unless you wanted the stock to be put to you.

If you sold the put in order to *have* the stock put to you (on expiration), you don't need to do anything except have the funds available in your account in order to purchase the stock. When the stock is put to you, your cost base would be $92.75 a share:

Stock's strike price when put to you	$95.00
Money taken in when you sold the put	−$ 2.25
Cost per share	$92.75

Remember, options technically expire on the third Friday of each month. However, the actual close out of options is at 12 P.M. (noon) on *Saturday.* This is important for you to remember, because many option investors assume that if the stock is above the strike price on the third Friday, then the stock won't be put to them.

However, this is incorrect. The stock *can* be put to you before 12 P.M. on Saturday, which is technically the expiration time, but you won't know for sure until the opening of the market on Monday. Say you sold the June $95 put and the stock closed on the Friday of expiration at $96—you might assume that the stock wasn't put to you. Guess what—after the close on Friday, the stock dropped in value below $95. You are now the proud owner of the stock at the $95 strike price.

In Chapter 3 we discussed disciplined trading, and this is a perfect example of learning to discipline yourself to buy back

---

If you can dream it, you can do it.

—Walt Disney

the put you sold. If there's no time left, all you'd be paying for would be the intrinsic value (the difference between the $95 strike price and the actual stock price before the close). Use your own trading judgment—if you think the stock is high enough and won't drop below your strike price by the Saturday 12 P.M. expiration, then you may allow the option to expire worthless.

Pay close attention to your investments! If you don't treat your trades like a business and watch your business investments, you could end up losing a lot of money. It's important for you to know what your investments are doing. The further the stock drops, the more money it will cost you to buy back the put. A great Web site for selling puts is www.writingputs.com.

Now that you understand selling puts, lets talk about *buying* puts. Buying puts is the opposite of selling puts. When you sell a put, somebody has the right to put the stock to you. When you buy a put, you have the right to put the stock to someone else.

By buying a put, you acquire the right to put the stock to someone at a certain price on or before the expiration date. Let's say that the June $90 put cost was $1.25 per share, and 10 contracts (1,000 shares) cost $1,250. At the time you bought the June $90 put, the stock was trading at $92. By buying the put, you gained the right to put the stock to someone else for $90 on or before expiration. If the stock was then trading above your $90 strike price, you wouldn't sell the stock to someone for less than what it was worth. In this case, your option would expire worthless and you would lose your $1,250.

Buying puts is just the opposite of selling puts, giving *you* the right to put the stock to someone at the selected price if the stock is worth less than your selected strike price. You'll

---

One life; a little gleam of time between two eternities; no second chance for us forever more.

—Thomas Carlyle

find that many investors buy put options for the sole purpose of selling the option for a profit.

If a company has bad news and the stock begins to drop in value, you would buy the put option, and then sell the option for a profit as the stock drops in value. When buying put options, the premium increases in value as the stock value drops further below your strike price.

Example

Option	Total Contracts	Premium per Share	Total Cost
June $90 put	10 (1,000 shares)	$1.25	$1,250.00

When you bought the June $90 put, the stock was trading at $92 (out of the money by $2). You made this investment because you had researched certain factors that could result in the stock dropping below the $90 strike price. You were right, and as the stock dropped in value your option went up in value. So, using the preceding example, let's say the stock dropped to $84 on expiration of the June options. You now have the right to put 1,000 shares of stock to someone for $90 per share, if you own the stock. And, if you own the option, you could sell the put option for a profit. If you own the stock, your profit would be $4,750. You figure this by first multiplying $90 per share (the price you have the right to put the stock to someone for) times 1,000 shares owned. Subtract from this $84 per share (the current stock value) times 1,000 shares, leaving $6,000. Finally, subtract the $1250 out-of-pocket cost to buy the $90 put, leaving $4,750.

People seldom improve when they have no model but themselves to copy after.

—Oliver Goldsmith

If you bought the put and do not own the stock, your second choice would be to sell the option and keep the profit. Your profit from just trading the option would be about the same, $4,750. Just remember, options consist of two parts—time value and intrinsic value—and market makers may offer less for selling the put option.

Hopefully, you now clearly understand the difference between buying and selling puts. In a bull put spread, you sell the higher-strike-price put, and buy a lower-strike-price put. When choosing strike prices, remember to be sure that the stock price will close above the strike price on expiration. When you sell puts, you receive the premium for that strike price, but when you buy the lower put, you will have to spend money for that strike price. This is considered to be a *credit spread,* receiving the net difference between the selling and buying cost. Figures 11.1, 11.2, and 11.3 show confirmation slips for bull put spreads with the net credit. This is also the total profit if the stock remains above the higher strike price.

The purpose of a bull put spread is to sell a put and buy a put at the same time, usually during the same phone call to your broker. Let me explain the benefits before showing you an actual example. When you sell the put, you receive the premium in your account, and the stock will be put to you if it is trading below that specified strike price on expiration. When you buy the lower strike price, you spend money and have the right to put the stock to someone on or before the expiration.

When buying or selling options—or, for that matter, when investing in the stock market—it's always better to limit your risk. If the stock will be put to you on or before expiration, then why not have the right to put the stock to someone else to

---

The first step towards success in any occupation is to become interested in it.

—Sir William Osler

Figure 11.2 Confirmation slips of Microsoft Corporation (MSFT) bull put spread trades

Quantity 10		Price 7 1/4	Settlement Amount	
Description: PUT MICROSOFT CORP OPENING UNSOLICITED TRADE	AT 95 EXPIRES 06-20-1998		Principal Commission S.E.C. Fee Trans Fee Net Amount	$7,250.00 100.86 0.25 7.00 $7,141.89 **SOLD**
			Security No. 1D803 Symbol PMSQJN95	

You Bought
Trade Date 05/14/98 for Settlement on 05/15/98

Quantity 10		Price 4 3/8	Settlement Amount	
Description: PUT MICROSOFT CORP OPENING UNSOLICITED TRADE	AT 90 EXPIRES 06-20-1998		Principal Commission H/P/I Trans Fee Net Amount	$4,375.00 82.90 2.35 7.00 $4,467.25 **BOUGHT**
			PROFIT $ 2,674.64	
			Security No. 1D800 Symbol PMSQJN90	

A good mind is lord of a kingdom.

—Seneca

Figure 11.3 Confirmation slips of CMG Information Services (CMGI) bull put spread trades

SIPC

CMG INFORM SERVICES

MEMBER NATIONAL ASSOCIATION OF SECURITIES DEALERS, INC. & CHICAGO STOCK EXCHANGE

ORIGINATOR	ACCOUNT NUMBER	TRANS. NO.	TR.	*CAP	SETT.	AR	TRADE DATE	SETTLEMENT DATE	ENTRY DATE
C 001		344-1083	087	3-D		J	12/10/98	12/11/98	

TAX I.D. NO.	CONTRA PARTY		SYMBOL	SPECIAL DELIVERY INSTRUCTIONS.
			QGCXN.	

ACCOUNT OF:
OR SPECIAL
DISPOSITION

	QUANTITY	CUSIP NUMBER	SECURITY DESCRIPTION	NET AMOUNT
YOU SLD	10	1257509XN	PUT -CMG INFORM SERVICE DEC 70 12/19/1998	3,433.88 SOLD

OPENING TRANSACTION   UNSOLICITED ORDER

PRICE	PRINCIPAL AMOUNT	INTEREST	* COMMISSION	TAX OR FCF	MISC.	S.E.C. FEE	A-E
3 1/2	3500.00		62.50		3.50	.12	R R1

Stocks and Bonds
CONFIRMATION

SIPC

MEMBER NATIONAL ASSOCIATION OF SECURITIES DEALERS, INC. & CHICAGO STOCK EXCHANGE

ORIGINATOR	ACCOUNT NUMBER	TRANS. NO.	TR.	*CAP	SETT.	AR	TRADE DATE	SETTLEMENT DATE	ENTRY DATE
C 001		344-2528	087	3-D		4	12/10/98	12/11/98	

TAX I.D. NO.	CONTRA PARTY		SYMBOL	SPECIAL DELIVERY INSTRUCTIONS.
			QGCXM.	

ACCOUNT OF:
OR SPECIAL
DISPOSITION

	QUANTITY	CUSIP NUMBER	SECURITY DESCRIPTION	NET AMOUNT
YOU BOT	10	1257509XM	PUT -CMG INFORM SERVICE DEC 65 12/19/1998	2,053.00 BOUGHT

OPENING TRANSACTION   UNSOLICITED ORDER

PRICE	PRINCIPAL AMOUNT	INTEREST	* COMMISSION	TAX OR FCF	MISC.	S.E.C. FEE	A-E
2.00	2000.00		47.50		5.50		D R1

PROFIT $ 1,380.88

Moderation is the key of lasting enjoyment.

—Hosea Ballou

cover your position in case the stock value ends up trading for a loss to you?

Example

Sell the June $95 put and receive the $2.25 per share.

Buy the June $90 put and pay out $1 per share.

Let's use our favorite example of 10 contracts (1,000 shares). If you sell 10 contracts, you receive $2,225 *into* your account. You then buy 10 contracts, and your cost is $1,000 *out of* your account. You have now created a bull put spread (you are bullish on the stock), and by the third Friday of June you will profit $1,225 if the stock is above the $95 strike price.

Your *margin requirement* is the difference between the strike price of the put you sold and the put you bought. In this example, the difference between $95 and $90 is $5 per share; for 10 contracts, that's $5,000. The absolute worst scenario would be one in which someone put the stock to you for $95 regardless of how much lower the stock was, and, in return, you put the stock to someone for $90 regardless of how much lower the stock was. If you were to buy and sell fewer contracts, then the margin would be less. As an investor in the stock market, you should know what the risks are, and what your potential losses could be.

If you're going to trade bull put spreads on stock splits, *maximize your return.* If you are bullish on a stock, then you are most likely going to be bullish on a stock-split announcement, with the positive news potentially driving the stock up. Once again, be sure to choose the right strike price so that the odds of the stock staying above that price are in your favor.

Here are my thoughts on good news and stock splits.

There is only one duty; that is to be happy.

—Denis Diderot

When good news, such as a stock split, is first announced, market makers and specialists are quick to inflate the call options. I like to take advantage of this and create a bull put spread. But I like to maximize my spread, which then creates a larger profit for my account. I refer to this as *legging into a spread* (selling the put quickly, then buying the put after the stock runs up).

Upon the announcement of the good news, I quickly sell the put for my chosen strike price. In doing this as fast as possible I am able to receive the maximum dollar amount for that strike price. As the news gets out, the stock price goes up and the market maker reduces the premium in the put I've sold. Once I have confirmation that I have sold the put, I tell my broker to wait before buying the underlying put.

When the news is released, the market makers will reduce the premium price on the buying side of the puts as the stock rises upward. I like to wait for the stock to reach a maximum price on the news announcement and then buy the next-lower-priced put. The higher the stock rises, the less I will have to pay to buy the put. This creates a larger credit spread, which puts more money in my account.

Example

The stock price is $87.

	Jumping In	*Legging In*
Sell $90 put	$3.50	$3.50
Buy $85 put	$1.50	$1.00
Profit per share	$2.00	$2.50

If I can put one touch of a rosy sunset into the life of any man or woman, I shall feel that I have worked with God.

—George MacDonald

I use the term *jumping in* for the method in which you quickly sell the $90 put and then immediately buy the $85 put, creating a bull put spread netting $2 per share. The term *legging in* describes the method in which you place one trade at a time instead of simultaneously. The difference is timing. By legging into this example, you would quickly sell the $90 put on the news and then wait for the news to drive the stock value up, which in this case lowers the $85 put from $1.50 to $1.00. You would have thus legged into a bull put spread and allowed the positive news to work to your advantage. Another common play is *legging out* spreads (closing out a spread one leg at a time).

You can buy the lower leg of the spread whenever you choose to, but I usually make sure to buy the underlying put the same day the stock hits a high point. If you don't buy the put the trading day prior to the close of the option market, you will have created a naked position. Creating a naked position is very risky and requires a lot of margin.

If you have the buying power and margin capability, then you can choose to buy the put at any time before the expiration date of the put you sold. However, you will find that when you implement this strategy correctly it is wise to buy the put on the same day. Most of my bull put positions are covered within 15 minutes of the release of the positive news or stock-split announcement.

You don't need to spend all your time on the phone with your broker. Give your broker the discretion to fill your buy position before the stock starts pulling back down and the market makers and specialists start putting the premium back into the put you'll be buying (as stock prices drop in value, put options increase in value). If your broker won't do this for you,

---

The first rule is not to lose. The second rule is not to forget the first rule.

—Warren Buffett

then place a limit order to buy the put at a lower price. Be sure to check before the close of the market to see if the limit order has been filled. If it has not, then it would be wise to buy the put to cover the position, thus creating a bull put spread.

In Chapter 6 we covered the terms *in, at,* and *out of the money.* To cover these concepts here with bull put spreads, I would like to say that you should always paper trade first, and as time goes on you will find the difference between the strike prices and different credit spread profits.

The key, not only to bull put spreads but to all trades, is to take a profit when you can and find another play. If the stock runs drastically higher than the upper leg of your put at anytime during the trade, close out the trade and free up the margin requirement. This is the exact opposite of selling the upper leg. You buy back the same strike price and month option. If the stock has a nice upward run, the cost of the put should be minimal, given that there isn't a lot of time premium left in the option.

Say your spread is going well. The stock has risen above the $95 strike price and is now currently trading at $98. You have one week left before the expiration. One choice you have is to wait for the expiration and let the option expire worthless, netting you the premium of $1,225. Your other choice is to close out the spread for a little less, knowing you can take the profit now. Let's take the profit off the table and move on to the next trade. To completely close out the spread, you will buy back the $95 put (upper leg) you sold and then sell the $90 put (lower leg) you bought.

Your cost to close out a spread depends on two things: how much the stock has risen above the $95 and $90 strike

---

*Be such a man, and live such a life, that if every man were
such as you, and every life a life like yours,
this earth would be God's Paradise.*

—Phillips Brooks

Figure 11.4   Analyzing the bull put spread

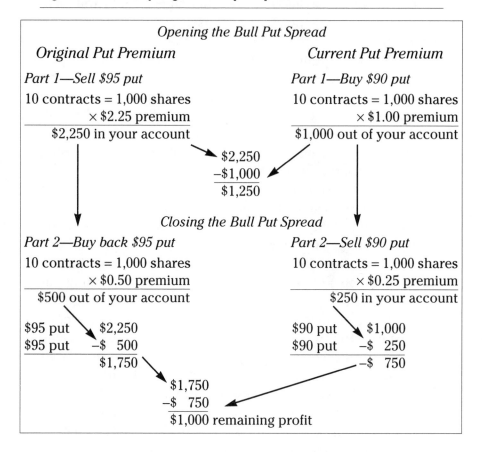

price, and how much time remains until the option's expiration. To determine this, let's use Figure 11.4 to see if it's financially beneficial.

When originally placing the spread, the premium received was $1,250 (selling the $95 put), but in order to close the $95

---

*To understand and to be understood
makes our happiness on earth.*

—German proverb

put as shown in Figure 11.4, you would have to buy back the $95 put for $500, leaving you the difference of $750. You have now closed out the position and assured yourself that the stock can *not* be put to you for $95 per share.

Let's discuss your advantages with the $90 put, which you originally bought when opening the bull put spread. At the time, the premium you paid was $1,000, and now you're going to completely close out the spread, so you will sell the $90 put, which is worth $250. By adding the $750 from before (the $95 put) and the $250 (the $90 put), your total profit (after closing out the spread) is now $1,000.

I've briefly explained this so that if you need to close out your spreads you can and should, especially if you believe that there is a possibility of bad news affecting the value of the stock. Or, you may just choose to leg out of your spread if you believe that the stock is going to drop much lower than the bottom leg ($90 put) of your spread. This is done by closing out the upper leg ($95 put) and holding on to the lower leg ($90 put). Remember, investors buy put options with the anticipation that the stock will drop in value, which increases the value of their options. If you're placing bull put spreads on stock-split candidates, you should understand that stocks have a tendency to pull back after the release of the news. By holding the lower leg, you are increasing your chance of making money if the stock pulls back below that strike price ($90 put). You have closed out the upper leg of the bull put spread and you are holding the lower leg, which is the put option that you bought. The further the stock drops below your $90 put price, the more the option increases in value.

This strategy is great to use with company earnings, as the stocks tend to run up in value a few days prior to the

---

No mistake or failure is as bad as to stop and not try again.

—John Wanamaker

Figure 11.5   Practice sheet for paper trading bull put spreads

BULL PUT SPREAD
SIMUTRADE RECORD PRACTICE TRACKING SHEET

Stock _Microsoft Corp._ Ticker _MSFT_   Price $ _91.00_
Top Leg Put _95_   Contracts _10_   Price $ _7,250.00_
Bottom Leg Put _90_   Contracts _10_   Price $ _4,375.00_
     Credit Amt. $ _2,875.00_
Date Spread Expired _6/20_   Profit = Credit = $ _2,875.00_
Date Assigned _/_   Loss = Spread - Credit = $ _∅_

Stock_____ Ticker_____ Price $_____
Top Leg Put _____ Contracts_____ Price $_____
Bottom Leg Put _____ Contracts_____ Price $_____
     Credit Amt. $_____
Date Spread Expired _/_   Profit = Credit = $_____
Date Assigned _/_   Loss = Spread - Credit = $_____

Stock_____ Ticker_____ Price $_____
Top Leg Put _____ Contracts_____ Price $_____
Bottom Leg Put _____ Contracts_____ Price $_____
     Credit Amt. $_____
Date Spread Expired _/_   Profit = Credit = $_____
Date Assigned _/_   Loss = Spread - Credit = $_____

Stock_____ Ticker_____ Price $_____
Top Leg Put _____ Contracts_____ Price $_____
Bottom Leg Put _____ Contracts_____ Price $_____
     Credit Amt. $_____
Date Spread Expired _/_   Profit = Credit = $_____
Date Assigned _/_   Loss = Spread - Credit = $_____

Stock_____ Ticker_____ Price $_____
Top Leg Put _____ Contracts_____ Price $_____
Bottom Leg Put _____ Contracts_____ Price $_____
     Credit Amt. $_____
Date Spread Expired _/_   Profit = Credit = $_____
Date Assigned _/_   Loss = Spread - Credit = $_____

Stock_____ Ticker_____ Price $_____
Top Leg Put _____ Contracts_____ Price $_____
Bottom Leg Put _____ Contracts_____ Price $_____
     Credit Amt. $_____
Date Spread Expired _/_   Profit = Credit = $_____
Date Assigned _/_   Loss = Spread - Credit = $_____

release of earnings and then sell off as investors take some profits. Great examples of this can be seen with a good charting service.

I have done my best to simplify the bull put spread strategy; now it is up to you to start paper trading the strategy so you can start using your green money (see Figure 11.5). Bull put spreads are not complicated: Sell the higher strike price and then buy the next lower strike price, creating the net debit. If the stock is trading above your higher strike price upon expiration, you keep the premium you received between the put sold and the put bought. Don't make it any more difficult for yourself than that. See the confirmation slips in Figures 11.1 to 11.3.

Figure 11.5 shows a tracking sheet used to practice paper trading. Don't start using real money until you fully understand not only when to enter a trade but, more important, how to exit the trade if need be. Your success will be determined by your knowledge.

The stock market is an exciting place to do business, as long as you have the knowledge. I urge you to continue your education by reading and studying as much as you can. (The proper knowledge and investments can be an important key to life.) Create a network of investors who trade in the stock market using the same strategies that you use, and never give up on your dreams.

The mightiest works have been accomplished by men who have kept their ability to dream great dreams.

—Walter Bowie

chapter 12

conclusion

In conclusion, let's review the previous chapters and refresh your memory as you begin to pursue your financial dreams. When investing, always remember your sole purpose for investing and what you are trying to accomplish. Know your purpose for placing each trade, and know when to exit the trade. Whether they are for the sake of helping your family members, helping your church, saving for your children's college education, or saving for your retirement, the only way you'll accomplish your investment goals is by never forgetting the value of the dollar and what it is able to do for you and your family.

We are drowning for information but starving for knowledge.

—John Naisbitt

Don't lose perspective on the market, and always remember that the stock market can be a dangerous place—when given the opportunity, the stock market will take advantage of you. The stock market will outlive us all, so never think that you have to make a trade or you'll miss out on an opportunity. Investors lose opportunities only when they have financially taken themselves out of the market because of greed or a lack of investment knowledge. Investments should be made after thorough research and evaluation of charts. Any consistent investor will agree that wise investments are rewarded with financial freedom—which, in turn, allows one the freedom of being able to do what one chooses, when one chooses to do it.

Investing in the stock market is a *business* and should be regarded as your own personal business. Remember the rules of being in business, what your business objectives are, and how you're going to go about accomplishing your financial business objectives. Put together a yearly business plan—and stick to the plan. Know why you are buying or selling certain inventory (i.e., investments)—and know when to hold your investments versus when to sell them. Remember that all businesses have losses—but the successful businesses are those that know when to cut their losses and take a *minimal* loss, not a total loss. You must remember that the true risk in option trading is the fact that the options can expire worthless if they don't perform within their expiration dates.

Always be in control of your money, and never assume that it's safe to let someone else make your decisions. Consulting with educated investors is recommended. Just remember that you have your own best interest at stake in your investments—no one else does. No one can feel your pain or experience your financial loss like you can. Power is

---

If it ain't broke don't fix it.

—Burt Lance

not the issue, but control is important. The point is that all investors should always know what investments they hold and the value of their accounts. Many investors take things for granted and only look at their year-end statements. Successful businesses operate within a standard of business rules and guidelines.

The most important rule of business is never to get too *greedy.* Focus on taking a lot of small profits. Practice your skill at buying wholesale and selling retail, keeping in mind always to predetermine your exit point prior to your entry into an investment. Home Depot buys goods only at wholesale prices in order to capture a predetermined retail profit. Always know what your bottom-line net profit will be. Negotiate your commissions, and remember the value of each dollar as it puts you $1 closer to your financial goal. As times change in the financial arena, investment firms will and should charge a fee based only on the net profit of one's account, also taking into consideration one's volume of annual trading. As a society, we should get back to paying for services solely based on the dollar amount of investors' profits, not their losses. An investor who trades regularly and shows an annual profit models a true win-win situation—both the brokerage firm and the investor can continue to enjoy a profitable lifelong business relationship.

Properly prepare yourself for the market by practicing with the white money, not the green money. Fully understand the strategy (know why you are making the investment), and practice continuously until you reach the point of winning on 7 out of 10 trades. Remember that it's *perfect* practice that makes perfect. You can practice something over and over and still not get it right if it's not done perfectly. A perfect trade results when an investor follows these four rules:

When prosperity comes, do not use all of it.

—Confucius

- Know why you are investing in a certain company.
- Know when is the right time to enter the trade.
- Know when to exit the trade for a profit.
- Most important, know when to limit your losses.

When you allow yourself to follow these important steps, you position yourself to take the final investment step and figure out the rate of return on your investment. Staying focused on your rate of return and not the dollar amount on your investment is a key factor in determining how successful your investing will be. Remember that it's always possible to maximize your return and limit your losses when you use the proper tools of trading. Once the trade has been placed, your most valuable tools are the good-till-canceled (GTC) order, the stop-loss order, and the trailing stop-loss order. Never consider trades to be complete unless you have placed the GTC and stop-loss orders at the initial time of your order placement. As for the trailing stop loss, it's nothing other than moving your stop-loss order up to maximize your profits and protect your investment against an immediate change in direction, allowing for a predetermined exit point on the downside.

Cash in on the analysts and develop your knowledge of which brokerage firms and ratings can drive the value of a stock up or down. As an investor you should always be aware that what an analyst says about a company can greatly affect the value of a stock's performance both in the short term and the long term. The two most common ratings used by all analysts are upgrading or downgrading a stock. The obvious choice of the two ratings is the upgrade. Upgrading a stock can create both a short-term and a long-term *increase* in the stock's

---

A purpose is the eternal condition of success.

—Theodore T. Munger

value. Downgrading a stock can create both a short-term and a long-term *decrease* in the stock's value. More favorable ratings are when the analyst puts a future price value with the rating. When this is done, the analyst is stating that the predicted stock value can reach a certain stated price within a certain time frame, which is 12 months for most ratings. Refer back to Chapter 4 and the brokerage firms' equity ratings systems presented in Figure 4.1 for a better understanding of brokerage firm ratings.

Charting your way to profits is nothing other than understanding how to review a chart on a particular stock, enabling you to determine when the best time for entry into a position may be—or, just as important, when the best time to exit the trade may be. As the saying goes, a picture in the stock market is worth thousands of dollars. Consider charting as having the same value as reviewing X-rays with your doctor prior to surgery. You wouldn't allow a surgeon to operate on you unless they reviewed the X-rays with you. The same should go for your investments: Don't make the trade without viewing the chart.

Charting offers many different ways to help one determine not only which investments would be best, but also the right timing of the investments. The most favorable charting indicators are the: balance of power, moving average, money stream, stochastics, and candlestick indicators. The worst indicator for charting is an investor who doesn't review a chart. Understanding charts is no different to an investor than reviewing an X-ray is to a surgeon. The key point is *knowledge*. TeleChart 2000 offers free charting classes throughout the country. Get the knowledge and enhance your trading ability.

Option investing offers many different opportunities that aren't available when investing solely in stock. However, remem-

---

The purpose of life is to believe, to hope, and to strive.

—Indira Gandhi

ber that investors of the old school will remind you that option investing is *risky.* Once again, I'm making a public statement by saying that I do agree that option investing is risky—but to what *degree,* I ask.

Let me remind you that the *only* risk to option investing is that you can lose your entire investment when you make the wrong decision. Now ask yourself the following question: Is this any different than buying a stock that then drops in value? Okay, the only point that the antioption investors have is that the stock can go back up in value if you hold onto it long enough. I could argue the pros and cons of both option investing and stock investing at length; however, until the day comes when investors seek to get the proper knowledge on option investing, I'll be fighting a losing battle.

Let me give you an example. Recently I began working on research for a future investment book, and I made three appointments with three separate large brokerage firms. (No names are given in due respect to the old-school way of thinking.) During my appointments I was interviewing the superior at each of these three large firms, and I questioned them about when a brokerage is allowed to trade options for itself or for its customers. Their answer to my question was *never.* I even went so far as to ask about selling naked puts in order to purchase a stock at a discount price. Again, the answer was *never.* Truly, their concern about the *risk* of any option investing is that the customers may elect to hold the firm responsible for customers' losses. Well, I believe the same would apply if the losses were due to purchasing stocks.

My point in this explanation is that investors should understand what they're doing and always stick to the rules of option investing. Remember the importance of stop-loss orders; GTC

It is better to say, "I don't know," than to lie about it.

—Ignas Bernstein

orders; in-the-money, at-the-money, and out-of-the-money options; intrinsic values; and time values. Truly, I'm a believer that anyone who can pick a blue-chip stock should make money within a reasonable amount of time. As for an option investment, it takes more dedication and research to ensure that you pick not only a good blue-chip stock, but more so, the right option.

Options can be conservative, as well. A good example would be a long-term equity anticipation securities (LEAPS) option. Say an investor was interested in buying a stock like General Electric (GE). As an investor, I would be investing for the purpose of catching the upside gain. When buying the stock, one would anticipate that the stock would go up by a certain percentage within two years. As an option investor, I would expect the same of the stock. I would rather purchase the call option (the right to buy or sell the stock for a certain price on or before a certain date). Why choose the LEAPS option rather than buying the stock? To purchase 1,000 shares of GE at the current cost of $150 per share, my investment would be $150,000 ($150 × 1,000 shares). However, if I were to purchase 10 contracts of the January 2002 $150 call option, my investment would be only $35,750. Truly, an option investor has many advantages in this situation:

- You have the power of leveraging your money. By investing in the call option, your out-of-pocket investment is reduced by $114,250.

- You still have the right to buy the stock at any time prior to the expiration of your two-year option.

- You control the same amount of stock as the investor who spent $114,250 more then you did.

Life is either a daring adventure or nothing.

—Helen Keller

- You now have the ability to diversify your remaining investments into other good blue-chip stocks.
- Your out-of-pocket risk is limited to the original investment of $35,750, rather than $150,000.

All five reasons can be justified if you believe in one thing as an investor—that the stock value will increase within the next two years. Remember that you also have three choices between the date of purchase and the expiration of the option:

- You can exercise your right to buy the 1,000 shares of stock at the set strike price of $150. (Add it to your blue-chip portfolio.)
- Prior to the option expiration you can sell the option, taking your profits or limiting your losses if the stock turns bearish.
- You can generate a monthly income (implementing the option strategy known as the calendar spread), which will reduce the cost base of the option (or the cost base of the stock, if you elected to purchase the stock).

Based on the examples shown here, you may now understand why investors have an incentive to acquire more knowledge in order to understand options and how options can benefit investors. The most favorable attraction of option investing is the ability to trade with less money and still have the capability of taking part in the more expensive stocks. As a rule of thumb, beginning option investors should limit their option trades solely to LEAPS options. After gaining a better

---

Everything comes too late for those who only wait.

—Elbert Hubbard

understanding of options, the next step would be to trade options based on news events such as the following:

- Preearnings bullish stock movement
- Preannouncement of a company stock split (Strategy 1)
- Announcement of stock split (Strategy 2)
- Dipping undervalued calls (DUC) play on a split announcement (Strategy 3)
- Pre-stock-split run (Strategy 4)
- Post-stock-split run (Strategy 5)
- New FDA drug approvals
- Potential company takeover (always investing in the company being acquired)
- Strong upgrades by reputable analysts
- Release of new favorable products

When playing these 10 bullish investments, the companies that are more predictable are those that have a consistent pattern of splitting their stock.

Before we begin reviewing the first five stock-split opportunities, let's review what a stock split is and its meaning to the investors in the company. Stock splits are nothing other than a way of distributing company profits to the shareholders. The two most common ways for shareholders to receive the company profits are through the disbursement of stock or the quarterly earnings. One large advantage to the disbursement of stock is the fact that it is not taxed until the time the stock is

---

*There is only one success: To be able to spend your life
in your own way.*

—Christopher Morley

sold, whereas the disbursement of the company profits in the form of a quarterly check is taxed in the year of acceptance.

Let's review the first five opportunities for company stock-split investments. First of the five is Strategy 1, the pre-announcement strategy. This strategy consists of dedicated research and proper execution. Nine out of every ten companies that split their stock have the tendency to revert back to their presplit stock price. By using TeleChart 2000 you can determine the price range of the stock prior to the announcement. A common pattern for a company's stock-split price is the price range of its previous split. Once you've determined the possible split price, your next step is to research the 14A proxy filing to ensure that the company has enough stock available. After completing your research, plan your execution, and select the option strike price and month. Be sure your option has plenty of time to allow for the announcement of the split. A poor option investment is one that expires worthless. Proper research will enable you to identify the potential split date while assuring yourself that your option has time remaining. Once the announcement is made, you should exit the trade when your GTC order to sell is executed.

The only difference between Strategy 1 and Strategy 2 is timing. With the presplit announcement, you open the trade several weeks or days prior to the announcement; with Strategy 2, the announcement strategy, you open the trade the same day as the split announcement is made. Most important, you close out both trades within minutes of the public announcement of the stock split. Always take into consideration that the ratio of the stock split will help determine the upside potential of your investment. The most favorable split ratios are 4 for 1, 3 for 1, and 2 for 1. Investors like to receive more in return on

To desire not to be anything is to desire not to be.

—Ayn Rand

their investments. A good example was the 4-for-1 split ratio offered by Qualcomm (QCOM).

Strategy 3, the postannouncement DUC play, is a trade of timing. Stocks have a tendency to drop in value shortly after the hype of the announcement, and investors then begin to take profits off the table. You should be standing on the sidelines as well, using your charts to determine when and at what price the stock will reestablish a new support line. The most important indicator will be the date the split actually takes place. The shorter the time frame between the announcement and the split date, the shorter the price drop can be. After the stock shows patterns of an upward reversal for three consecutive days, your plan of execution will be to select the option strike price and, more important, the expiration month. Longer-term options allow you to maximize your investment through Strategy 4 if the stock shows continuous signs of upward movement. Wise investors will utilize trailing stop losses to maximize their upside potential and limit their risk of giving back profits if the stock doesn't continue upward. Knowing that you still have the opportunity to reinvest for Strategy 4, be careful and pay close attention to resistance levels which are normally the price range close to the same price at the time of the announcement.

Strategy 4 is the presplit run. This strategy is mind boggling to many investors, yet the presplit run can be very rewarding. Positioning for the bullish upside of this trade is made within three to five days *prior* to the actual split, otherwise known as the ex-dividend date. The mind-boggling part of this strategy is the reason behind the run up of the stock just

---

*Sooner or later, a man, if he is wise, discovers that life
is a mixture of good days and bad,
victory and defeat, give and take.*

—Wilfred A. Peterson

prior to its split date. As I research this play over and over, it still appears that investors create the increase in the stock's value only because those who buy the stock want to take advantage of the stock-split dividend. For buying investors, this ex-dividend day is the last trading day to purchase the stock in order to receive the increase in stock shares. Yet it's no different then waiting until the next trading day, when the stock price is reduced in consideration of the current split ratio.

An example: As of the close of the market on the ex-dividend date, the stock's last trading price was $80 per share and the split ratio was 2 for 1. The new trading price as of the next market day would be one-half of the last trading price, or $40 per share. The actual value of the stock does not change, just the number of shares an investor owns. In a 2-for-1 stock split, the investor would now own two shares for every one share owned prior to the split. Yes, you could still receive the same benefit if you were to purchase twice as many shares at the $40 price after the split.

This is a great short-term trade that enables you to get in and out of the trade within three to seven days. Ideally, it's best to sell your option on the final day prior to the split or sooner. Many of the stock-split companies have a tendency to sell off once the new split ratio takes effect. This is common, as many large hedge funds sell out of their positions and take their profits. As profits are being taken, the stock starts to drop in value for a period of time until it establishes a new support level. This drop in value brings us to the fifth trade of stock splits, the postsplit DUC play.

The postsplit investment is by far the most rewarding trade of these five strategies. I'll even go as far as to say that it's my favorite option trade. Once you've located a stock that shows

No man will work for your interests unless they are his.

—David Seabury

consistent patterns of stock splits, you can take advantage of the upside potential when purchasing long-term options. These options are known as LEAPS. LEAPS options are available one and two years out. For example, if the current month were February 2000, I could buy LEAPS options for the years 2001 and 2002. Remember that LEAPS are written only for the month of January. When a LEAPS gets to the point of having less than six months until expiration, it's no longer considered a LEAPS option. In the case of this example, in July 2000 the 2001 LEAPS becomes a normal option as the LEAPS options for the year 2003 become available.

When researching LEAPS prices, you'll note that they can be very expensive because of the options time value. However they are still a lot less expensive than buying the stock. Knowing when to purchase the LEAPS is not as important as with the preceding four stock-split strategies. LEAPS options allow some room for error only because time works for you, allowing the stock either one or two years to perform. Ideally, the proper entry point of this trade will be after the sell-off following the split has taken place and the stock has tested a good support level. As for which strike price to choose, again you can't make too big of an error as long as the stock returns to its previous split price within your allowed expiration time.

Personally, I prefer to buy one or two strike prices out of the money (the out-of-the-money option is when the stock is trading lower than the strike price of the purchased option). When trading out-of-the-money options, you'll find that the cost of the option is lower, enabling you to have less money at risk or giving you the opportunity to purchase more contracts. Keep in mind that LEAPS options are call options, enabling the buyer of the option to profit as the stock value increases dur-

---

In making a living today, many no longer leave room for life.

—Joseph R. Sizoo, DD

ing the time frame of the option. As with any call option, the buyer has the *right,* not the *obligation,* to do one of two things:

- Sell the option at any time prior to its expiration.
- Exercise the right to buy the stock for the chosen strike price.

Note: As the buyer of the option, you can sell as little or as many contracts as you choose, at any time you choose, prior to the expiration. The same applies to the purchase of the stock: You can exercise your right to buy as few or as many shares as you wish, as long as you own the option. However, the stock can be purchased only in increments of 100 shares, equaling the same amount for each contract (option contracts are bought, sold, or exercised in 100-share increments). Table 12.1 lists companies that have a history of splitting their stock.

Take time to review each chart, and you'll see the pattern and stock-split indicators showing how often the company splits its stock. Stock splits are like the stock market in general, offering investors no guarantees. However, more research can determine predictability based on the company's history and stock performance. If you find that you yourself are an investor who prefers to buy the stock rather than the option, then review the same information and locate those companies that split their stock more often.

Don't forget that option investments are treated just like the stock—when the stock splits, the option splits in accordance with its split ratio, too. For example, in the case of a 2-for-1 split ratio, one $80 call option will split in half and become two $40 call options. And the same applies to your

---

Minds are like parachutes—they only function when open.

—Lord Thomas Dewar

Table 12.1 Companies with a History of Stock Splits

Company Name	Ticker Symbol	Company Name	Ticker Symbol
Amazon.com	AMZN	IBM Corporation	IBM
America Online, Inc.	AOL	Intel Corporation	INTC
BMC Software	BMCS	Jabil Circuit, Inc.	JBL
Broadcom Corporation	BRCM	JDS Uniphase	
Broadvision, Inc.	BVSN	Corporation	JDSU
Check Point Software		Juniper Network	JNPR
Technology	CHKP	Lucent Technology	LU
CMG Information		Microsoft Corporation	MSFT
Services, Inc.	CMGI	Microstrategy	MSTR
Commerce One	CMRC	Nokia Corporation	NOK
Comverse Technology,		Oracle Corporation	ORCL
Inc.	CMVT	Qualcomm, Inc.	QCOM
Cisco Systems	CSCO	Red Hat, Inc.	RHAT
Dell Computer	DELL	Real Network	RNWK
Doubleclick, Inc.	DCLK	Sun Microsystems	SUNW
E-Bay	EBAY	Vignette Corporation	VIGN
EMC Corporation	EMC	Wal-Mart	WMT
Home Depot, Inc.	HD	Yahoo!	YAHOO
Hewlett-Packard	HWP		

cost. If your cost for the option was $12 per contract, it will split in half and become $6.

From an investment point of view, the LEAPS options are no different from owning the stock, as long as the stock has that consistent pattern of returning back to its previous split value. Purchasing LEAPS options allows for diversifica-

---

Plan ahead: It wasn't raining when Noah built the ark.

—Richard Cushing

tion into several companies and allows for a great return on your money. Due to the long time frame of the investment, this postsplit strategy is also known as the range rider strategy— you patiently wait as the stock value increases and rides its way up the range back to the top. Remember not to get to caught up on the premium you'll pay for LEAPS—the largest percentage (or possibly all) of the premium you'll pay will be for the *time value*. When investing in LEAPS you always pay more for the time value than the *intrinsic value*. Of all option trades, this is the only trade that works in your favor if the stock drastically drops in value.

Yes, option prices will drop in value. However, you will not suffer as much of a loss in comparison to the actual dollar amount of the stock. Remaining time in your option is very valuable, because it can enable the stock to retrace its upward trend, increasing the option premium. Market makers take this into consideration, and knowing the past performance of the company, they are reluctant to drop the option price equally in conjunction with the stock price. As a beginner in the options market, you should start with LEAPS option and focus on the longer-term performance of those companies listed in Table 12.1.

Let's finish our review by highlighting Strategy 6, a more advanced strategy known to investors as bull put spreads. The term *bull* indicates that the investor is bullish on the stock and believes that the stock's value will increase within a reasonable amount of time. The "reasonable amount of time" is in reference to the expiration date of the option, which should be the shortest expiration date available. Bull put spreads do have a predetermined amount of risk associated with them; however,

---

Poverty is not disgrace to a man,
but it is confoundedly inconvenient.

—Sydney Smith

the risk of loss can be much greater if your trading options are any further out than 30 days. The ideal time for implementing a bull put spread is about 2 weeks (10 trading days) or less of the current option month.

Implementing bull put spreads is an investment of strategy, and it *does* require research. Thorough research is a must because the option expiration time is so short, not allowing you much time or room for error if the stock drops in value. You should not invest in bull put spreads if the stock value doesn't have a certain positive news item or purpose to increase its value. Stock splits are positive news and can be a good reason to consider placing a bull put spread. Such positive news items as strong earnings reports, FDA approval of new products, and bids for corporate takeovers can be reasons for considering bull put spreads, too.

Once you've completed your charting research and have been able to identify the bullish indicators shown in the money stream, balance of power, and support and resistance levels, your next decision is to determine what combination of strike prices you are going to *sell* and *buy*. The bull put spread consists of implementing two option trades at the same time. The most important option will be the *put* option you'll be *selling*. This selected strike price *must* be your elected price, which the stock value will remain above come the expiration of your option. When selling the put option, you will receive a premium for doing so. Now you must *buy* a put option equaling the *same* number of contracts you sold. Just the opposite of receiving a premium when you sold the put option, you're now *paying* a premium to buy the put option. The ideal put option to buy is the *next lower* strike price below the put option you sold.

---

*Practice in life what you pray for, and God
will give it to you more abundantly.*

—Pusey

Once you have *sold the higher* strike price and *bought the lower* strike price, you subtract the difference between the premium you took in and the premium you paid. You now have a credit spread, which is your profit.

As long as the stock remains above your higher selected strike price on expiration of the options, there's no need for you to do anything, and no additional commission will be charged. Looking to the downside of the trade, your loss will be the dollar amount between the price difference of the two selected strike prices multiplied by the number of contracts you traded.

For example, let's say you selected the upper strike price of $80 and the next lower strike price of $75. This is a difference of $5 per contract. Your maximum margin requirement and potential loss would be $500 per contract. Let's review the steps of bull put spreads:

1. You are bullish on the stock (research indicates an upward movement in the stock value).
2. Select the shortest option expiration available (longer expiration can increase the risk).
3. Select the upper leg of the option first (the strike price you're going to sell).
4. Select the next lower option price, known as the lower leg (the strike price you're going to buy).
5. Determine your potential profit (net difference between the option you sold and the option you bought).
6. Come the expiration of your selected option, keep your profit and pay no additional commissions as long

---

You are financially secure when you can afford anything you want and you don't want anything.

—Art Buck

as the stock price is above your selected upper-leg option.

Following these six steps is easier than it might appear. Don't try to get creative with bull put spreads—or, for any matter, with any strategy. Strategies have a purpose, and they work best when the rules of the trade are *always* followed. Experimenting with proven strategies increases your risk and reduces your profit potential. As your knowledge and experience grows, you may chose to play both directions of a bull put spread and close out either the upper or lower leg if you can identify a drastic movement in the stock value to either the upside or downside. It's important to remember that any time you sell a put option and don't own the underlying option, you've put yourself in what is known as a *naked position*. As the saying goes on Wall Street, don't get caught running around naked—it can be a very embarrassing and expensive mistake. Invest wisely and conservatively: Don't create a bull put spread if the stock doesn't show a positive sign of increasing value.

We've reviewed the basics of all 11 chapters, including the 6 different investment strategies that can be implemented by either a stock or an options investor. Select your favorite strategy, remember to follow the rules as they are, and *practice* until you truly understand what you're doing—and, more important, identify your *purpose* for making the trade.

I wish you the best of success in all of your trades. But more important, I pray that God will bless you and your family by allowing you to venture on to a more profitable and rewarding lifestyle.

God does not want us to do extraordinary things: He wants us to do ordinary things extraordinarily well.

—Bishop Gore

Glossary

ask price   The current price for which a security may be bought (purchased).

asset allocation   How assets are diversified between various investments—stocks, bonds, real estate, and so on.

at the close   The last price a security trades for when the market stops trading for the day.

at the money   Used to describe an option whose strike price is the same as the stock price.

at the open   The price a stock security trades for when the market begins trading for the day.

balance of power   A technical indicator developed by Worden Brothers that is designed to show patterns of systematic buying and selling by informed buyers.

bearish   Used to describe a trading environment which the market is declining.

bear spread   In futures and options trading, a strategy in which one contract is bought and a different contract is sold in such a manner that the person undertaking the spread makes a profit if the price of the underlined asset declines.

bell   The device that sounds to mark the open and close of each trading day on an organized securities exchange.

best ask   The price at which a market makers who own a security offer to sell it; also known as the *ask price*. The lowest quoted offer price of all competing market makers to sell a particular stock at any given time.

bid/ask spread   The difference between the price at which a market maker is willing to buy a security (bid) and the price at which the firm is willing to sell it (ask). The spread narrows or widens according to the supply of and demand for the security being traded.

bid price The current price at which a security could be sold. The bid is the price at which market makers are willing to buy a security. In general, the bid price is always lower than the asking price.

Big Blue A widely used reference to IBM Corporation. The term derives from the company's logo, which usually appears in blue.

Big Board A widely used reference to the New York Stock Exchange.

Big Three A widely used reference to the three major automobile manufacturers in the United States: Daimler-Chrysler, Ford, and General Motors.

Black Monday A widely used reference to October 19, 1987, the day the Dow Jones Industrial Average dropped a record 508 points, nearly 23 percent.

Black Thursday A widely used reference to October 24, 1929, the day when security prices plunged, producing one of the most memorable days in the history of the New York Stock Exchange.

block trade Usually, a trade of 10,000 shares or more. For bonds, a face amount of $200,000 or more. Block trades are often executed through a special section of a brokerage firm called the *block desk*. Using the block desk may result in a better price.

blue chip Generally used to refer to securities of companies having a long history of sustained earnings and dividend payments.

board of directors The group of people responsible for supervising the affairs of a corporation. This group is also responsible for the decision to split the company's stock.

bottom fishing Used to refer to the activity of investing in securities when it is believed that the market has reached bottom following a major decline.

breakaway gap   In technical terms, a gap in a chart pattern of price movement indicating that a stock price has broken out of a trend on high volume.

breakout   The advance of a stock price above a resistance level, or the fall of a stock price below a support level.

broker   An individual or firm that brings together buyers and sellers but does not take a position in the asset to be exchanged. In the broadest sense, an agent who facilitates trades between a buyer and a seller and receives a commission for this service.

bull   An investor who believes that the price of a security or security prices in general will follow an upward trend.

bullish   Relating to the belief that a particular stock or the overall market is headed for a period of generally rising prices.

bull spread   In futures and options trading, a strategy in which one contract is bought and a different contract is sold in such a manner that the person undertaking the spread makes a profit if the price of the underlying asset rises. Two contracts are used in order to limit the size of the potential loss. Bull spreads are used both for call and put options.

buying power   The funds in an investor's brokerage account that may be used for purchasing securities. An investor's buying power includes cash balances plus the loan value on securities held in the account.

buy signal   An indication provided by a technical tool, such as a bar chart or trading volume, that a particular security or securities in general should be purchased.

buy stop order   A customer's order to a broker to buy a security if it sells at or above a stipulated stop price. This type of stop order can be used to protect an existing profit or to limit the potential loss on a security that has been sold short.

called away Used to describe stock taken (sold) away from an option seller because the stock was at or above the strike price on the third Friday of the expiration month.

call option An option contract, giving the owner the right (not the obligation) to buy shares of stock at a strike price on or before the expiration date. The investor also has the right to sell the option for a profit before the expiration of the option. The buyer of the underlying stock is speculating that the underlying stock will go up in value, hence increasing the value of the option.

call price The price an investor pays when purchasing the call option, giving the investor the right to buy stock for a certain price (also known as the *premium*) on or before the expiration date of the chosen option.

call spread The result of an investor buying a call on a particular security and writing a call with a different expiration date, different exercise price, or both on the same security.

cancel order A customer order to a broker that cancels an earlier, unfilled order given by the customer. A canceled order can be used when buying or selling.

cash account An account in which a client is required to pay in full for securities purchased by a specific date from the trade date. Cleared funds must be in the account within three business days to cover any purchases.

chasing a stock Buying or shorting a stock after it has already made a large move. Chasing a stock is considered very dangerous, because one may buy at the top or short the stock at the bottom.

Chicago Board Options Exchange (CBOE) A securities exchange that was established in 1973 as the nation's first organized floor for trading standardized options. Although its success spawned option trading on a number of other exchanges, the CBOE remains the most active options exchange in the country.

circuit breaker A procedure that temporarily halts trading on all U.S. stock markets for 1 hour when the Dow Jones Industrial Average falls 250 points or more within a trading day. The pause is designed to allow time for the markets to absorb the news that precipitated the decline. Should the average fall another 150 points within the same day, trading would again be halted, this time for 2 hours.

Class A/Class B shares Shares of stock issued by the same company but having some difference, such as voting rights, a dividend preference, or participation. Class B shares are normally the less desirable shares and can also be less expensive.

CLO At the close. A CLO order will be executed as near the closing price as possible. Note that the closing price is not guaranteed as the purchase or selling price.

common stock Security representing a partial ownership interest in a corporation. Ownership may also be in shares of preferred stock, which has a prior claim on any dividends to be paid and, in the event of liquidation, to the distribution of the corporation's assets. Common stockholders assume the primary risk if business is poor, and realize greater gains in the event of success. They also elect the board of directors that controls the company.

contract In options trading, an agreement by the writer either to buy (if a put) or to sell (if a call) a given asset at a predetermined price until a certain date. The holder of the option is under no obligation to act.

contract size In futures and options, the size or amount of an asset to be delivered. For example, stock options nearly always specify 100 shares, while a silver futures contract on the Chicago Mercantile Exchange stipulates 5,000 troy ounces.

covered call writing A transaction in which an investor who owns stock sells a call option against that stock, giving the buyer the right to take the stock if the stock value is above the strike price of the call sold upon expiration of the option. Upon expiration, if the stock value is below the strike price of the call option sold, the investor keeps the premium received when selling the call. The writer of the covered call makes a profit or loss on the stock that is called away, depending on the purchase price (the cost base).

covering   Getting out of a short position. When one is short in a stock, one needs to buy back the borrowed shares to close out the trade. This can create either a profit or a loss to the investor, depending on the cost of the stock at the time it was shorted.

credit spread   The simultaneous sale of one option and purchase of another option that results in a credit to the investor's account. Thus, more funds are received from the sale than are required for the purchase.

current market value   The value of an individual's portfolio when the securities are appraised at current market prices. This may vary when using a margin account.

current ratio   A company's current assets divided by its current liabilities. This ratio is commonly used by many long-term investors to determine the strength of a company.

day trade   A trade that is opened and closed the same day.

day trader   An investor who buys and sells stock the same day and, win or loss, is fully back to cash by the market close on that day.

delayed opening   An intentional delay in the opening transaction of a particular security. Generally, the delay occurs when unexpected developments occur before the opening, making it difficult for the specialist to match buy and sell orders.

delta   The change in the price of an option that results from a 1-point change in the price of the underlying stock. For example, a delta of 0.5 indicates that the option will rise in price by ¹/₂ point (50 cents) for each 1-point ($1) rise in the price of the underlying stock. Call options have positive deltas; put options have negative deltas.

diagonal spread   Any spread with different strike prices in which the purchased options have a longer maturity than the written options.

dip   A small, short decline in the price of a security.

discount brokerage firm   A brokerage firm that discounts the commissions it charges to individual investors to trade securities. Most discount brokerage firms offer limited advice, but their fees are 50 percent or less of those charged by full-service brokerage firms.

discretionary account   Written approval by an investor giving a money manager the right to buy or sell securities at the manager's discretion, without a prior contact, as long as established parameters are followed.

dividend   A share of a company's net proceeds distributed by the company to its stockholders. The amount is decided by the board of directors and is usually paid quarterly.

double witching   Used to describe the day when both options and futures expire.

Dow Jones Industrial Average (DJIA)   A trademark for one of the oldest and most widely quoted measures of stock market price movement. The average is calculated by adding the share prices of 30 large, seasoned industrial firms, such as IBM, Exxon, AT&T, and General Motors, and dividing the sum by a figure that is adjusted for such things as stock splits and substitutions.

downgrading   A reduction in the quality rating of a security by brokerage firms. Downgrades can affect the value of a stock creating a drop in the price of the security. Certain downgrades by certain brokerage firms have different effects on different stocks.

downtick   A drop in the bid price by one level to the next lower price.

downtrend   A series of price declines in a security or the general market.

earnings   The income of a business. Earnings usually refer to after-tax income but may occasionally be summarized with before-tax revenues. The value of a company's stock can be related to its earnings in each quarter of a year. Companys that continue to show strong earnings tend to be more favorable to most investors.

earnings per share (EPS)   An earnings measure calculated by subtracting the dividends paid to holders of preferred stock from the net income for a period and dividing that result by the average number of common shares outstanding during that period.

equity   In a brokerage account, the market value of securities minus the amount borrowed. Equity is particularly important for margin accounts, for which minimum standards must be met.

ex-dividend   Used to refer to a stock no longer carrying the right to the next dividend payment because the settlement date occurs after the record date. This is the date when a security begins trading without the dividend (cash or stock) included in the contract price.

ex-dividend date   The first day of trading when the seller, rather than the buyer, will be entitled to the most recently announced dividend payment. Also used to refer to the date after which the stock purchaser is not entitled to the current quarterly dividend.

exercise price   The dollar price at which the owner of an option can force the writer to sell an asset (call option) or to buy an asset (put option).

expiration date   The last day on which an option holder may exercise an option. This date is stated in the contract at the time the option is written.

fill-or-kill (FOK) order   An order sent to the floor of an exchange, demanding that it either be filled immediately and in full or be canceled. It doesn't ensure that the order will be entirely filled at the same price.

foreign A company based outside the United States with securities trading on the Nasdaq stock exchange.

Form 10-K See **10-K.**

full-service brokerage firm A brokerage firm that provides a wide range of services and products to its customers, including research and advice. Their fees are higher than those of discount brokerage firms.

fundamental analysis (fundamentals) The study of a company's financial reports, marketing, management, and overall business characteristics as a means of determining the value of a stock.

gap opening The opening trade of a security in which the opening price shows a significant increase or decrease compared with that security's closing price of the previous day.

going public A practice by which a privately held company sells a portion of its ownership to the general public through a stock offering. Owners generally take their firms public because they need additional large sums of equity funding that they are unable or unwilling to contribute themselves.

good-till-canceled (GTC) order An order either to buy or to sell a security that remains in effect until it is canceled by the customer, or it is executed by the broker. Also known as an *open order.*

GTC Get the cash! (A strategy recommended by the author.)

halting A situation in which a security is temporarily not available for trading (for example, market makers are not allowed to display quotes). Halting of a security is common prior to or during market hourse when a stock value can be affected by either good or bad news.

Individual Retirement Account (IRA) A government-regulated retirement account plan in which contributions are tax-deductible and gains are tax-deferred.

initial margin requirement   The amount of equity a customer must deposit when making a new purchase in a margin account. Margin accounts apply to stocks but are not allowed for the purchase of options.

initial public offering (IPO)   The first sale of stock by a company to the public, commonly referred to as *going public*. A company making an IPO is seeking outside equity capital and a public market for its stock.

institutional investor   A bank, mutual fund, pension fund, or other corporate entity that trades securities in large volumes.

in-the-money   Used to describe a call (or put) option that has a strike price considerably less (or more) than the market price of the underlying stock. A deep-in-the-money option is also certain to be exercised on or before its expiration.

intrinsic value   The amount, if any, by which an option is in the money. This is determined by comparing the current trading price of the stock and the strike price of the option. The difference in value is the intrinsic value, or equity.

IRA   See **Individual Retirement Account.**

limit   An order in which the maximum price the investor wants to pay for the purchase, or a minimum price the investor will accept as a seller, is set. Limit orders can be used for buying and selling of both stocks and options.

long-term equity anticipation securities (LEAPS)   Long ownership of a stock or option; owning a security on which an option is written. An option with an extended expiration date, usually out one and two years, and written in January of those years.

long-term gain   A gain on the sale of a capital asset where the holding period is six months or more and the profit is subject to the long-term capital gains tax.

margin   The amount of equity as a percentage of one's current market value in a margin account.

margin account   An account in which a brokerage firm lends a client part of the purchase price of securities.

margin call   A demand for a client to deposit money or securities when a purchase is made in excess of the value of a margin account, or when the collateral (margin securities) goes down in value.

market maker   A dealer willing to accept the risk of holding securities to facilitate trading in a particular security or securities.

market order   An immediately executed order to buy or sell a stock or option at the best available price. The order may not be executed at the price the investor expected (Be very cautious, as market orders are normally not filled at the most desirable prices).

market value   The price at which an investor will buy or sell each share of common stock at a given time.

married put   A transaction in which an investor buys a stock and on the same day buys a put option on the underlying stock.

moving average   An average that moves forward with time, dropping earlier components as later ones are added. This is an analytical tool, which smooths out the fluctuations of a stock chart.

naked option   An opening transaction in an option when the underlying asset is not owned. An investor writing a call on 100 shares of IBM without owning the stock is writing a naked option. If the stock is called by the option holder, the writer must purchase shares in the market for delivery and is therefore caught naked.

naked position   A security position, either long or short, that is not hedged. For example, an investor short 500 shares of IBM with no other position in IBM stock (such as ownership of calls) has a naked position in that security. Because a naked position subjects the investor to large potential gains or losses, it is an aggressive investment position.

news driven   Any news about a security or stock that affects the volatility or the movement of that particular stock.

New York Stock Exchange (NYSE)   The trademarked name of the largest and oldest organized securities exchange in the United States. The NYSE, founded in 1792, currently trades about 85 percent of the nation's listed securities. Most large publicly traded firms' stock, including all those listed in the Dow Jones averages, list their stock on the NYSE.

nondiscretionary account   An account in which the client must give consent for any purchase or sale before the trade is made, either in person or by phone.

opening   The beginning of a trading session. The initial price at which a security trades for the day.

open order   An order to buy or sell a security that remains in effect until it is either canceled by the customer or executed.

OPG   At the opening. An OPG order will be executed at the opening price. If it is not executed at the opening, it will be canceled automatically.

option   The right to either buy or sell a specified amount or value at a fixed exercise price. An option that gives the right to buy is a *call option.* An option that gives the right to sell is a *put option.* The investor must exercise the option before the specified expiration date. Stock options expire on the third Friday of each month and can become absolutely worthless.

option cycle   The series of months during which option contracts expire. Options for a particular stock or index generally expire on the same four months every year, plus the current and following month.

option premium   The sum of money one pays for an option or receives for an option.

Options Clearing Corporation (OCC) An organization, established in 1972, to process and guarantee the transactions in options that take place on the organized exchanges.

order A customer's instructions to buy or sell securities.

out of the money Used to describe a call option with a strike price significantly above the market price of the underlying stock. A deep-out-of-the-money call or put option is priced significantly lower because in all likelihood it can expire worthless.

over the counter (OTC) A security that is not listed or traded on a major exchange.

paper trade A trade recorded and tracked, but not using actual funds in a brokerage account. This is done as a means of learning and testing strategy.

penny stock A low-priced, speculative stock.

pink sheets The daily sheets that contain the wholesale price quotations for thousands of over-the-counter stocks as listed by dealers who act as market makers in the individual securities.

position An investment stake in a security.

position trader A security trader who holds a position overnight, and, in some cases, for even longer periods.

premium Amount by which a bond sells above par; or, the cost of an option.

proxy The written authority to act or speak for another party. Proxies are sent to stockholders by corporate management in order to solicit authority to vote the shareholders' shares at the annual meetings.

publicly traded company A company whose shares of common stock are held by the public and are available for purchase by investors.

put option An option contract that gives the owner the right to force the sale of a certain number of shares of stock at a specified price on or before a specific date. Written only in increments of 100 shares per contact.

put spread   An investment in which an investor purchases one put on a particular stock and sells another put on the same stock but with a different expiration date, exercise price, or both.

range rider   A stock that has highs and lows on its price range and gradually rises to a high range over a period of time.

resistance   The upper level of a stock's trading range at which a stock's price appears to be limited in upward movement. This normally indicates that there are more sellers then buyers. Going through resistance is called a *breakout.*

retirement   The point in one's life when one no longer has to trade one's time for a paycheck (according to the author).

reverse stock split   An increase in the stock's par value caused by reducing the number of shares outstanding.

rolling options   A strategy of buying calls or puts on a rolling stock. Such a stock shows a consistent pattern of traveling up and down between two levels—the top level is the *resistance,* and the bottom level is the *support level.*

rolling out   A strategy of buying back an existing option (closing the position prior to its expiration) and rewriting with a different expiration date and strike price. Commonly used by investors selling naked puts who don't want the stock to be put to them.

round trip   Used to describe paying a commission on a buy-and-sell trade.

scalper   An in-and-out trader who attempts to profit on relatively small price changes. Commonly used by day traders.

short sale   The sale of a security that must be borrowed to make delivery. The investor borrows stock to sell from a brokerage house with hopes of repurchasing it at a lower price for a profit. This is regularly done by brokers when a stock can't justify its current high price or when an investor believes the market is showing signs of a sell-off.

short-term gain   The loss realized from the sale of securities or other capital assets held for six months or less.

specialist   A member of a securities exchange who is a market maker in one or more securities listed on the exchange. Specialists are assigned securities by the exchange and are expected to maintain a fair and orderly market on them.

spread   (1) A transaction in which the investor is both a buyer and seller of the same type of option, with the options having different exercise prices and/or expiration dates. (2) The difference between the bid and the ask for a stock or option.

stock   An instrument that signifies an ownership position in a corporation.

stock dividend   Payment of a corporation dividend in the form of stock rather than cash. The stock dividend may be additional shares in the company, or it may be shares in a subsidiary being spun off to shareholders. Stock dividends are often used to conserve cash needed to operate the business. Unlike a cash dividend, stock dividends are not taxed until they are sold.

stock split   The division of outstanding shares of a corporation into a larger or smaller number of shares. For example, in a 3-for-1 split, each holder of 100 shares would have 300 shares after the split, although the proportionate equity in the company would remain the same. A *reverse split* occurs when the company reduces the total number of outstanding shares, but each share is worth more.

stop-loss order   Sell order placed on a stock below the current market price. If the stock price falls below this price, it automatically becomes an open at-the-market sell order to prevent further loss.

stop order   An order to buy or to sell a security when the security's price reaches or passes a specified price.

strike price   The price at which the underlying security will be bought or sold if the option buyer or seller exercises their rights in the contract prior to the option's expiration date.

support level   The lower point of a stock's chart pattern, used as an indication of whether a stock can return to an upward direction or will break below its support level and drop in value. Typically this is a price at which there is more demand than supply; stock usually bottoms out because there are more buyers than sellers (for example, a stock sits just above $30, but doesn't go below $30).

suspended trading   The temporary suspension of trading in a security. Trading in a security may be suspended if, for instance, a major announcement by the issuing company is expected to significantly influence the security's price. The temporary halt in trading is intended to give the financial community enough time to hear the news. Also called a *trading halt.*

takeover   The acquisition of a controlling interest in a firm. Although the term is often used to refer to acquisition by a party hostile to the target's management, many takeovers are friendly.

10-K   An annual report on a firm's operations filed with the Securities and Exchange Commission (SEC). Compared to the typical annual report sent to stockholders, a 10-K is much less physically attractive; however, it contains many more detailed operating and financial statistics, including information on legal proceedings and management compensation. A firm's stockholders may obtain a free copy of the 10-K by writing to the corporate treasurer. Also called *Form 10-K.*

thin float   A small number of shares available for purchase or sale on the market. This can tend to drive the stock value up due to a lack of shares, which can create more demand.

tick   A movement in the price or price quotation of a security or contract.

ticker symbol   A trading symbol used by a company to identify itself on a stock exchange.

time value   Whatever the premium of the option is in addition to its intrinsic value.

trading halt   See **suspended trading.**

trailing stop   A stop order to sell (or buy) a security in which subsequent stop orders are placed at progressively higher (or lower) levels as the stock price increases (or decreases).

trendline   In technical analysis, a straight line or two parallel straight lines that indicate the direction in which a security has been moving, and, many chartists believe, the direction in which it will continue to move. When a security price breaks through a trend line, the beginning of a new trend is indicated.

triple bottom   In technical analysis, a chart formation of a stock or a market index that has attempted to penetrate a lower price level on three different occasions. If the stock price or index actually breaks through on the downside during the third attempt, it is a bearish signal and the investor should sell or sell short the stock or index. If the stock or index is unable to penetrate the price level, it is a bullish sign that the price is at a strong support level.

triple witching hour   The hour before the market closing on a day when options and futures on stock indexes both expire, thereby setting off frenzied trading in futures, options, and underlying securities. Traders and arbitrageurs unwind investment positions and produce large price movements in securities. The triple witching hour occurs on the third Friday of March, June, September, and December.

upgrading   An increase in the quality rating of a security issue. An upgrade may occur for a variety of reasons, including an improved outlook for a firm's products, increased profitability, or a reduction in the amount of debt the firm has outstanding. As circumstances change, upgrading or downgrading of a security takes place once the issue had been initially rated and sold. An upgrading generally can be expected to have a positive influence on the price of the security.

uptick rule   A Securities and Exchange Commission (SEC) rule that prohibits the sale of borrowed stock when the last price change in the stock was downward. Part of the Securities Exchange Act of 1934, the uptick rule is designed to keep investors from manipulating stock prices downward by borrowing and selling shares in a declining stock.

volatile   When speaking of the stock market and of stocks or securities, this is when the market or a particular stock's price tends to vary often and wildly.

volume   The amount of trading sustained in a security or in the entire market during a given period. Especially heavy volume may indicate that important news has just been announced or is expected.

Index